'This is the most practical, commonsense guide available to handling people problems in the workplace. Every supervisor and manager should have one.'

— Sherie Gravelle, Qantas Holidays Supervisor

'Laurie brings to this book his wealth of experience in conflict resolution, development programs and consultancy and has packaged it all as a user-friendly, real-world support book for anyone who has to supervise and manage people.'

— Jan Donaldson, Training and Development Manager, June Dally Watkins Pty Ltd

Also available in this series:

making it happen

making conflict resolution happen

A simple and effective guide to dealing with conflict at work

Laurie Dicker

ALLEN&UNWIN

First published by Allen & Unwin in 2002
First published in 2001

Allen & Unwin
83 Alexander Street,
Crows Nest, NSW 2065
Australia
Phone: (61 2) 8425 0100
Fax: (61 2) 9906 2218
E-mail: info@allenandunwin.com
Web: www.allenandunwin.com

National Library of Australia
Cataloguing-in-Publication entry:

Dicker, Laurie.
Making conflict resolution happen: a simple and effective guide to
dealing with conflict at work.

Includes index.

ISBN 1 86508 991 5

1. Conflict Management. I. Title. (Series: Making it happen).

658.4053

Acquisitions Editor: Tim Edwards
Copy Editor: Loretta Barnard
Text design: Peta Nugent
Printed by McPherson's Printing Group, Maryborough, Victoria

10 9 8 7 6 5 4 3 2 1

about
the series

making it happen

Are you committed to changing things for the better? Are you searching for ways to make your organisation more effective? Are you trying to help your people and organisation to improve, but are seriously strapped for time and money? If you are, then this Making It Happen book is written specifically for you.

Every book in the series is designed to assist change agents to get things done...to make new programs really happen...without costing the organisation an arm and a leg and without taking up all of your valuable time.

Each book in the series is written by a top consultant in the field who does not simply theorise about their subject of expertise but who explains specifically how to implement a program that will really work for your work unit or organisation. Vital advice on what works and what doesn't work, what tricks to use and traps to avoid, plus suggested strategies for implementation, templates and material to photocopy, and checklists to gauge your readiness — each book in the series is filled with useful information, all written in clear, practical language that enables you to make things happen, fast.

Help your people and work unit to increase their performance and love their work through implementing a program from the Making It Happen series and reap the rewards that successful change agents deserve.

about

the book

Over many years of analysing organisations, and from my experience in conflict resolution, I have found that the best operations have a middle management of change agents who have been willing to shift their leadership style to one that accepts that people are more important than tasks and functions. They accept that conflict and mistakes are inevitable and are exaggerated by the rate of change in the organisation, and they walk with their people in a cooperative, collaborative and cohesive unit, in an atmosphere of openness, honesty and trust towards a joint problem-solving approach to conflict resolution.

The most outstanding of these leaders develop a preventative approach to conflict by creating a working environment in which conflict is less likely to occur, or to develop to the extremes where it becomes difficult to manage. They develop a culture in which differences are recognised, valued and utilised for the benefit of all. They recognise that most conflict occurs because people are different and not necessarily because they are wrong. They see their role as managing the creative tensions that exist because of those differences and then leading them together towards progress and development.

Many supervisors and managers have the potential to deal effectively with conflict but have adopted a traditional approach of avoidance or negative sanction. This book will give you greater knowledge and understanding of the nature of conflict in the workplace and take you through a range of ideas and strategies for resolving issues. It will give you the courage and confidence to handle difficult situations and to shift to a management style that emphasises anticipation, early intervention and a joint, cooperative effort at resolution.

about
the author

Laurie Dicker, BA, MComm, DipT, is a management consultant specialising in conducting development programs in the areas of conflict resolution, negotiation, mediation, dealing with difficult people, change management, leadership, supervision, performance development, team building and career transition. He often works closely in-house with an organisation to design programs that are specific to their particular needs. He acts as a mediator and is sometimes called in by an organisation to assist with dysfunctional units.

Prior to setting up his own consultancy, Laurie was a Director of Human Resources responsible for HR and risk management for approximately 10 000 staff, as well as training and development, crisis management and industrial relations. He was also a member of a task force that implemented a major change management program in an organisation of 60 000 employees.

Laurie can be contacted through his email: dicker@smartchat.net.au

contents

chapter 1

Developments in conflict management

- Living and working with conflict
- Change and the conflict it creates
- Traditional approaches to conflict management
- Towards a joint problem-solving approach

■ LIVING WITH CONFLICT

Most conflict occurs because people are different, not necessarily because they are wrong.

Think about both the major wars and even the minor clashes between countries and the reasons why the people in those countries have been willing to kill each other in the cause of defending their rights and territory. The majority of wars are fought on the basis of differences, mostly of race, religion or political ideology. Although they may also fight over access to resources or territory, they will usually justify it on the basis of differences in race, religion or politics. Most of the people involved in a conflict between nations are good, law abiding citizens trying to get on with their lives, raise families and enjoy a happy, secure and stable lifestyle. But those same individuals will be willing to answer the call to arms and sacrifice their lives for their cause.

Think now of some of the conflict or grievance situations in which you have been involved or that you have witnessed both in your personal life and at work. How many of them have involved situations in which the other person or group has a significant difference from you? Is it because they are a different gender? Men are from Mars; women are from Venus. Or do the differences relate to such issues as age, race, religion, sexuality, language, culture, education, physical size or appearance, intellect, possessions, attitude, style of operation, power, authority, influence, wealth, status, access to information, access to resources or opportunity?

Alternatively, think of the number of times that you or the other person have created a conflict situation in order to establish or confirm a distinct difference or advantage in social or professional status, availability of resources or access to vital information. When was the last time you got very angry with someone? How often have you slammed your hand on the table in disgust or frustration at another person's statement or action? What were the circumstances that caused you to act in that manner? Have you ever stormed out of a room in anger rather than put up with the other person in there? When was the last time you argued or clashed with your partner, parents, children, a shop assistant, your boss, neighbour, flat mates, employees, police, banks, taxation authorities, someone on the sporting field or someone in the traffic?

Look to the dictionary and thesaurus for the words which relate to conflict — contrariness, absolute difference, mutual exclusiveness, antipathy, antagonism, opposition, clash, contradiction, opposite poles, opposing tendencies, contrast, fight, struggle, collision, incompatibility and opposing principles. All of these increase anxieties, the flow of adrenalin and the heart rate in anticipation of the need to fight or escape quickly to avoid hurt, injury or death. Because of the potential stress involved, people tend, in most cases, to avoid conflict or to put it aside. Sometimes they will display overt aggression in order to frighten away any potential opposition in much the same manner as dogs do as they run along the fence barking fiercely at any possible intruder. Do you have barking dogs in your organisation? Are you a barking dog?

Conflict can occur in a situation in which there is an incompatibility in a relationship, a difference of values, actions, thoughts, expectations or principles; it can be an event that can result in a fight, struggle, clash or collision of mind or body. Conflict can result in avoidance and separation or it can bring people closer together. Conflict is inevitable and is part of everyday life at home, at work or in the community, and the manner by which it is resolved is one of the most critical factors in any relationship.

Conflict is a situation in which two or more people or parties compete for limited status, power, information, influence, resources or territory. It emanates from a desire of one or both parties to have or acquire something that the other one has. It occurs when one tries to change the status quo, and by so doing, gains an advantage. Conflict is an inconsistency in attitudes and actions between two parties and results in competition for limited resources. These resources might be physical, financial, communicative, ideological, political, legal, psychological or emotional.

DIVERSITY

Conflict is an inconsistency in social attitudes and may result from a perceived or real inequity in the distribution and availability of resources. It will emerge as one feels the necessity to defend one's territory, whether that be personal, family, sport, work or on a national scale.

Conflict will emerge as a result of differences such as:

- intelligence, thinking skills and the capacity to reason and analyse
- personal qualities, charisma and personal power
- interpersonal qualities and the ability to get on with others
- physical attributes, appearance and health
- psychological and emotional well-being
- ability to perform physical tasks
- language and dialect
- ability to communicate
- status and titles
- cultural background, values and beliefs
- religion
- qualifications
- operational style or mode
- race
- colour
- political ideology
- gender and sexual orientation
- age
- access to legal advice and support
- financial support

- access to training and development
- access to information and the means by which it is transmitted
- living standards.

It's clear that conflict is inevitable whenever human beings interact. Unfortunately, most of us have not been comfortable talking about subjects such as gender, sex, sexual orientation, race, religion, politics and cultural differences because as children we were given clear messages that it was not right to talk about these subjects. They were not subjects for open discussion in public. As children we were told that it was rude to talk about such things.

> *'We don't talk about those things.'*
> *'Don't be a dirty little grub.'*
> *'For goodness' sake you've got a one track mind. Can't you talk about something else?'*
> *'It is not polite to discuss those matters.'*
> *'Don't ask people what they earn.'*
> *'They are not topics for children to talk about. Wait until you grow up.'*
> *'It's impolite to ask people who they voted for.'*

Even in adult life we have been warned not to raise subjects such as race, religion or politics when visiting other people's homes.

In most families there has also been a tendency to suppress discussion when differences lead to disputes.

> *'Stop arguing. I won't have you going on like that.'*
> *'Cut that out. What will the neighbours think?'*
> *'I don't have time to listen and that is not how decent children behave.'*

While, ideally, we would like life to very open, honest, transparent and played on a level playing field, this rarely happens. In the real world it is a very uneven surface and there are many significant differences between us.

But being different is not wrong. Being different increases the range of positive possibilities for change and development. Imagine how boring and static life and work would be if everybody was exactly the same and nobody ever questioned the status quo or made suggestions for improvement.

When we experience conflict we are usually troubled by it and are often confused about how to handle it. Often emotion can further cloud our thinking and hide the obvious path to resolution. This is as true for the workplace as it is in our personal lives.

Those who handle conflict best are those who accept it as a natural phenomenon in the family or work group and are open and honest in dealing with it, giving everyone an opportunity to work together to resolve their differences. The critical factor is how the conflict is resolved.

■ WORKPLACE CONFLICT

The workplace, like all aspects of life, consists of people who are different, and conflict in the workplace is a natural result of those differences as well as the changing environment in which people work. Consider all of the conflicts or grievances that have occurred in your workplace. They can be time-consuming and therefore costly for organisations that want to minimise the time spent on unproductive activities.

Think of why conflicts occur in your workplace. Try to avoid the traditional cliché of: 'We know they are always at each other's throats; but it is only a personality clash and there is nothing we can do.' There is little purpose in trying to treat a personality clash by separating or transferring the combatants. Shifting a person only shifts the problem. It is essential to deal with the underlying causes. A personality clash is merely a flashing red light warning you that there is a dangerous situation that must be addressed. You and I, who are directly involved with the supervision or management of people, can now lift ourselves above such excuses and explanations. We can look now for better ways of handling the resolution and management of conflict in a manner that will generate trust and confidence in our leadership and greater job satisfaction for those who work with us.

It is easy to be distracted by symptoms such as physical or verbal abuse, threat, harassment, coercion, confusion, ridicule, anger, argument, lack of communication, guilt, fear, resentment, rejection, regret, criticism, sickness and stress. Think about and assess the effect that these symptoms have on the effectiveness of outcomes in your area of work. Many managers complain that they spend most of their time dealing with the problems of only 10 per cent of their employees, clients and customers. Imagine how productive their lives would be if these problems could be resolved once and for all! In the real world, of course, this is wishful thinking. Problems and conflicts will continue to plague us. What causes difficult situations?

Most problems and conflicts in the workplace are caused by people who are considered difficult. Yet, at some time, each person in the workplace will be difficult to manage. They won't always follow our clear instructions; they will make mistakes; they will show emotions when you least expect it; they will question our management and they will generally place 'unreasonable' demands upon our limited time and resources. They also cause difficulties because they are not all the same; they don't act in concert; they require different degrees of support and guidance; they have different personalities, cultures, behaviours, language, race, gender, ages, senses of humour and styles of operation.

However, in every workplace, there are some whose behaviour and performance places them in the category of very difficult to manage — those who create the most conflict.

It is helpful to bear in mind the following points:

- Remember that in certain circumstances, each one of us is difficult. It is easy to look at the so-called 'difficult' characters with a holier-than-thou perspective but, when you look to the truth of your own behaviour, it is more realistic to get your feet back on the ground. While I am generally seen by others as a person who remains relatively calm in crisis situations and who is not prone to losing control, I will confess to you that there have been times and circumstances when I have behaved like many of these characters. What about you?
- You can learn from the situations in which you behaved similarly to the difficult person. Analyse the circumstances that caused you to act like them. If you can understand why you acted in that manner you will be better able to put yourself in the other person's shoes and come at the problem from their perspective. It will place you in a better position to walk beside them, instead of at them, towards resolution and agreement.
- Always be prepared for the unexpected. You might make assumptions based on past experience, but don't expect everyone to behave in the same way under all circumstances.

Example

Consider the problems that an Arthur Smarty has in the workplace and the conflicts that ensue from his presence. He is a know-it-all, adopts a superior attitude and uses his intellect to try to take control of you. He is condescending, aloof, sanctimonious, supercilious, snobbish, loves to belittle others and will try hard to crucify them publicly. He is stubborn and often bigoted, has the gift of the gab and can talk at length on any topic with a sense of authority. He is hypercritical and negative, quick to blame others if something fails and tries to make you feel inferior and insecure. He loves to grandstand at public meetings enjoying the attention he gets from others as he verbally takes you apart.

So, it is better to change our approach to managing conflict and to create a working environment in which problems are less likely to occur and in which the creative tensions are given an opportunity and encouragement for expression and development. Instead of trying to suppress, push aside or sanction an Arthur Smarty, try to identify his positive characteristics and potential. How could we better use those talents and redirect his energies to the benefit of the team? How will you change your approach to dealing with him?

As supervisors and managers, we understand the environment of difference that gives birth to, nurtures and promotes the growth of conflict. If we understand this basic principle first then we are in a better position to deal with the causes as well as the range of unacceptable behaviours that result from it.

The reality for us as managers is to recognise and appreciate the differences in the human and other resources in the organisation. Look to what each person has contributed or could contribute with positive support and encouragement. Look to the benefits and outcomes of those contributions and the potential it opens up for further development. Then manage the tensions and conflicts between those competing forces.

The best organisations are those that are a combination of differences — in skills, backgrounds, knowledge, experiences, genders, qualifications and values, together with a managerial attitude that attempts to combine those differences in such a manner that each will contribute to the other's development and gain from their association. Our prime responsibility is to coordinate and develop those differences, and to guide and mentor the creative tensions that will arise from those differences.

▶ **As managers we are in the people business and so the coordination and development of the people who report to us is our prime responsibility.**

■ CHANGE AND THE CONFLICT IT CREATES

As we move further into the 21st century, the rate of change in organisations is increasing, more in geometrical than in arithmetical proportions. Change increases uncertainty, which in turn nurtures anxieties, thus adding to the tensions that provide the compost in which conflicts grow. But the rate of change is not going to slow just because we are getting anxious. The global changes in organisations will continue, and at a faster rate than before.

Those of us who survive and progress in this atmosphere will be the ones who adapt our managerial skills and practices to meet the challenges of change through a better approach to managing conflict in the working environment. Change and conflict will not go away. They are both inevitable and will continue at an increasing rate. Be aware, however, that for every anxiety that is generated there will be at least an equal number of positive opportunities created. It is up to you and me to look for and take advantage of those opportunities and to better manage the stresses and conflicts that arise during the process.

We are now witnessing a dramatic change to the world of work and the economies in which that work takes place. We are in a period of volatility, ambiguity and what appears to be unreasonable disorder in which changes are increasingly different and inconsistent. Although it is not the same throughout all industries, there is a shift from traditional industrial modes of production towards more information technology and financial services. This trend is resulting in the decline or disappearance of traditional jobs and the emergence of a whole spectrum of new positions.

The shift towards a knowledge economy has increased investment in information systems and power struggles over the modes of information and their transmission. The fierce competition for scarce resources on a global scale and the strong push towards economic rationalism has resulted in organisations being in a continuous state of change and structural readjustment as they search for an economic advantage with reduced costs and increasing returns. How many times during the last 15 years has your organisation or part thereof been subject to restructuring, downsizing, outplacement, realignment, relocation, outsourcing, rationalisation or redundancies?

What impact have these changes had on the people at work? Some will adopt a siege mentality, locking down their current procedures and protecting their status quo, while others will sit idly, hoping that it will all go away after the new management has settled in. Who are the people who appear to be succeeding in the new changed environment? What are they doing to succeed? Look to those who are succeeding over an extended period, not just the flash in the pan types who are here today and gone tomorrow. What makes these people successful? How do they manage their staff? How do they deal with customers and clients? How do they handle difficult situations? How do they handle change?

> *Example*
> Consider the conflicts that occur in a period of change when there is a Blocker Barbara on the staff.
>
> 'No, no, no. Oh no, never. Over my dead body. You'll have a fight on your hands if that is what you think. With which letter are you having difficulty, the N or the O? Why change it?
> I can't see any sense in it. You will have a hard job convincing me. I don't see any benefit in it for me so I do not intend to do it. If it ain't broke don't fix it. I have sat in this chair for the last 15 years and have had 12 managers go through this section. They can keep coming through with their fancy ideas to get promotion but I ain't moving.'

Barbara is very stubborn and sees herself as the protector of past practice and the gate-keeper of the castle. She gets strength from resisting all attempts to change and will use a sharp tongue to protect her castle. She promotes anxiety in others about any change, develops a siege mentality that is hard to shift and will threaten action against anyone who tries to implement change. She creates conflicts with other staff and supervisors.

THE IMPACT OF GLOBALISATION

Increasing globalisation and freer world trade has significantly altered the nature and location of industries and workplaces. It is not uncommon to see large industries closed down and shifted offshore where costs are reduced, leaving hundreds of workers displaced and unemployed. Consider, for example, the changes in telemarketing. When you telephone what you believe to be the local office of a large corporation you are probably speaking to someone in another state or even in New Delhi, India, who does not even know where your town is located. Or worse still, the response will be a digital voice that does not even respond to your human frustration. Press button 9 to exterminate.

New products are appearing daily. It has been estimated that 60 per cent of the products and services that banks will offer in five years' time have not yet been developed and that 40 per cent of the jobs that will exist in 20 years' time do not exist today.

Organisations are now more flexible, adaptable, complex, mobile, universal and diverse. The workers in those organisations are more likely to be employed in short-term, temporary and contractual arrangements and on average will change jobs every three to four years. There will be fierce competition for the vacant positions in the organisation and an increased desire of quality staff to search for more promising opportunities elsewhere. There will be a marked decrease in the dedicated loyalty to the one organisation that existed in the last century.

The turbulence of these situations will create an increasing gap between the rich and poor, educated and less educated, skilled and unskilled, thus not only increasing the degree and range of differences between the people in the workplace, but also the potential for conflict and grievance.

Those who succeed will be more flexible, adaptable and committed to life-long learning, multiskilling and broadbanding their experiences. Those who will benefit from change will look for opportunities to be creative, developmental, vital, explorative, innovative, challenging and empowered and they will move into new areas of experience to explore, develop and test their potential.

Those who feel most threatened by these changes are those most likely to resist. They are more likely to be affected by the negative aspects of change such as anger, withdrawal, distress, anxiety, guilt, confusion, panic, loss of power and status, low self-esteem, aggression, resentment, fear, loss of confidence, sickness, absence, argument and destroyed relationships.

The challenge for you, should you be in the former group, will be to lead, guide and assist the others through the change process in a manner which makes them feel valued and empowered and helps them to make real contributions to their workplace and the organisation. By so doing you will be managing the differences and thus be better able to manage the conflicts that will arise from those differences. The question at this stage is: 'Do you have the essential characteristics to be an effective leader, manager or supervisor of people?'

■ TRADITIONAL APPROACHES TO CONFLICT MANAGEMENT

In the animal world there has always been fierce competition for scarce resources and a strong urge to propagate the species. For survival, animals have tended to adopt one or more of three main stances: to fight, to hide or to run. Under pressure, people tend to adopt the same strategies, although not always with the same intensity or life threatening immediacy. In a conflict situation, some will be aggressive, some will walk away and make themselves inconspicuous, while most will run away to avoid any involvement in the conflict situation or its resolution. Look to your own work situation and identify where each person generally fits into this framework. Who are the aggressors, who hides and who walks away to avoid the situation? How do you react in most cases to a conflict situation?

Who are the people in your personal and working life who adopt a fourth position: that of the mediator or conciliator who takes charge of the situation and works with the disputants towards resolution and agreement? When a crisis occurs, who are the people who always step in, take charge and manage the situation calmly and effectively? What is it that they have that clearly identifies them as being able to handle these situations?

Observe other people in your organisation to note those situations where people adopt a particular defensive approach to a difficult situation, such as storming out, having tantrums, bursting into tears, playing the victim, fantasising, moralising, making excuses, rationalising, being obsessive, threatening, blackmailing, preaching, delaying, withholding information or passively resisting. How often do you witness physical, verbal or emotional headbutting?

Organisations do what their name suggests: organise. They therefore establish and become enmeshed in a framework of laws, rules, regulations, policies and procedures. While this is necessary to establish a logical and systematic pattern of operations in organisations, it has also dominated the manner by which disputes have been settled. Managers tend to look more to the processes than they do to the people concerned in the dispute, because rules and regulations are more concrete and tangible and so, in most people's mind, more easily measurable and defensible.

Traditional dispute settlement has tended to take on a legal persona that, by its very nature, is adversarial, emphasises rights and wrongs, tries to establish guilt and innocence, polarises the differences between the parties and concludes with sanctions and penalties.

Under these circumstances not only is the conflict very stressful and destructive, but the process of resolution is negative and punitive. This traditional approach has tended to be very directive and coercive and while it might achieve quick results it rarely satisfies the parties involved in the dispute. These traditional approaches to conflict have been more in the context of power plays, headbutting and survival of the fittest. They are seen as the quickest, easiest and least costly method of solving disputes but, in the long term, rarely result in agreement or satisfaction in the disputing parties. They merely interrupt the process of conflict that will then resume at a later date and maybe in another place.

MANAGING PEOPLE INSTEAD OF TASKS

When most of us first entered the workforce we were very much involved in tasks, functions, procedures and products. We were guided in most cases by clear policies and guidelines. During those early stages of our career it was our job to complete a number of these actions to a desired quality in the given period of time and with an expected output. As we became more experienced we developed higher order skills and were able to carry out our tasks more efficiently. When we did this well and it was looked upon favourably by our supervisors there was a strong possibility that we were promoted.

At first this elevation involved only a higher number and range of tasks but, eventually, it involved the supervision, management and development of staff, clients and customers. At first we still tended to concentrate on the tasks and processes with which we were accustomed and expected others to do likewise, with some guidance where necessary. At this early stage of supervision it was difficult to let go of the tasks that we had been doing very efficiently. Some supervisors felt they had to continue to prove their superiority in task completion to justify their higher position, status and salary and forgot that their highest priority now was the management and development of people.

When things went wrong and conflicts and grievances occurred, their easy answer was to blame the staff for being inefficient and not being able to follow the clear guidelines that had been outlined. As the conflict developed further, remedial action tended too often to be a clarification of the tasks and time lines rather than dealing with the issues of people management. Too often then the dispute developed into an explosion or dysfunction from which point it was very difficult to regain control and development. At that point many supervisors passed it on to senior management or the human resources unit to 'fix'.

This traditional approach to management is one of **reaction** and tends to follow this pattern.

REACTION MODEL

In the reactive problem-solving model you:
- Wait until the problem occurs.
- Avoid direct involvement until it develops further.
- Deal with the problem by trying to improve tasks, functions and processes.
- Wait for further problems to occur.
- Adopt a crisis management model.
- React to the crisis.
- Address it after the event (post-operative).
- Try to reduce the inflammation.

- Try to apply a cure or bandaid.
- Try to shift one or more of the conflicting parties because of personality clashes.
- Apply sanctions and penalties to those believed to be involved.
- Make sanctions punitive as a lesson to them and others.
- Reclarify the roles, responsibilities, tasks, functions, processes and expected outputs.

Why do so many of us, especially in our early experiences as supervisors or managers, adopt this negative, destructive approach to problem-solving and difficulties? We normally rationalise or make excuses about these reactive approaches because we believe that the tasks, functions, processes and product are the most important aspect of our responsibility and because they are the more tangible items by which we and others can measure our success. We know that we are enthusiastic, energetic and are willing to work hard to achieve our functional targets and so it is easy to convince ourselves that we do not have time to deal with these other matters.

One of the most common statements of managers is: 'I spend most of my time cleaning up the problems of a few members of staff, difficult clients and customers and this interrupts the important work I am supposed to be doing.'

Mary

Mary is an extremely hard-working, dedicated, loyal and trustworthy supervisor/ manager. She was promoted to the position of manager because she was willing to put in that extra effort and was dedicated to the accurate completion on time of tasks and functions. She was always willing to enhance her own development by attending courses.

Mary is a perfectionist and is intolerant of sloppiness. She is proud of her high standards and the fact that she has so often been praised above others. She is conscious of the need to keep up her standards and becomes stressed when she sees that the quality of outcomes from her colleagues and staff is not up to hers. She gets much satisfaction from finding faults in the system and proving that she knows more about the technology than her supervisors. She delights in proving others wrong. It gives her a warm feeling when she can show her superiority in this way.

Mary has high expectations of her staff. She will provide information to those who show their dedication and loyalty to her. She is extremely demanding and intolerant of the supervisors who report to her and will often berate them in front of staff. In many instances she finds that it is much easier to do the work of others, because she is more capable and makes fewer mistakes.

She finds the work of the manager increasingly stressful because more staff question her policies and make suggestions for change. She sees this as disloyalty and has asked senior management either to terminate their services, demote them or

*transfer them elsewhere. She is intolerant of those who do not show the same
dedication as herself and distances herself from those who question her operations.*

*She now holds no formal staff meetings because she felt they gave staff too much
of an opportunity to be critical and questioning. She communicates with most staff
via written memos and email. Staff are becoming more disillusioned even though they
recognise that she has great intellect and skills in the financial area. She clings to
her tasks, functions, processes and manuals with the tenacity of a pit bull terrier and
uses them as her security blanket to justify her style of management.*

Without intervention by others what will be the most likely outcomes for Mary and her
section? How does this environment produce the conditions where conflict is more likely
to occur? Given the opportunity, what advice would you be giving to Mary? What has to
happen for her section to become a cooperative, cohesive, positive and productive unit in
which conflicts, disputes and differences are managed effectively?

As you mature as an effective leader, you will tend to move through stages. In the earlier
years you will adopt either a stand off and avoid position or one that is very directive and
coercive. Both these positions show signs of relative immaturity in handling conflict. The
first will attempt to establish distance from the conflict in the hope that it will sort itself
out or go away, while the other will jump in boots and all for a quick settlement. The first
avoids making real decisions; the latter makes coercive, directive, arbitrary decisions.

In the early stages managers are looking for **solutions** to conflict — anything that will
make it go away. They do this by making arbitrary decisions that they expect will be
carried out without question. But conflict is rarely ever solved through this process. What
you believe to be a solution will be your attempt to create a different set of circumstances
that usually in the long-term will lead to conflict recurring in a different framework.

As we mature and realise that quick arbitrary solutions are not the answer, we tend to
look more to outcomes which at least hint at a **settlement** of the dispute. This suggests
that the disputing parties at least have an opportunity to put their case before a decision
is made. The manager feels comfortable that everyone has had an opportunity to be
involved. The leader will listen and then decide on or recommend an appropriate action.
But it still will not solve the problem, because rarely do the disputants contribute to the
outcomes. They are recipients rather than contributors.

In recent years there has been a strong movement towards alternative dispute
resolution procedures with a key focus on the involvement of the parties in reaching
agreement to the outcomes. These approaches are outlined in Chapter 4. The emphasis
of these approaches is the attainment of an **agreement** to which both parties contribute
and are committed. They effectively have ownership of the outcomes. These approaches
tend to use a conciliatory or mediation approach or a variation of either to encourage the
conflicting parties to work together to come to an agreement with a facilitator or third
party to assist when necessary.

Today, the best managers work more using a **joint problem-solving approach** that emphasises collaboration, participation and the empowerment of the people concerned. To do this they have to shed the overt trappings of power, status, titles and position and replace them with the higher orders of influence and motivation. By adopting this approach you, the leader, will be more able to gain the cooperation of the participants, encourage them to walk together in an atmosphere of trust, empower them to be involved in the research and analysis of alternative options, and then guide them to agreement.

■ TOWARDS A JOINT PROBLEM-SOLVING APPROACH

The supervisors and managers who deal with conflict most effectively are those who shift their managerial style and direction to one that will emphasise the following.
- Acceptance that people are more important than tasks, functions, processes and product.
- An open acceptance that conflict is inevitable.
- A commitment to working together towards resolution.
- Walking with their people instead of at them.
- Recognition that change and conflict situations will provide opportunities for development.
- Collaboration, cooperation, cohesion.
- Development of trust, openness and honesty.
- Encouragement of participation and empowerment.
- Clear, varied and effective communication.
- Acceptance that we all make mistakes.
- Early anticipation and resolution of grievances.
- Effective teamwork involving sharing, guidance, support, development and mentoring.
- Establishment of a culture in which differences are recognised, valued and utilised for the benefit of all.
- Recognition and reward for achievement.
- Recognitionn that there is a joint involvement and responsibility in problem-solving.
- Working in support teams.
- Ensuring that the culture of support crosses team boundaries.

When you and others work together with mutual trust you will know that you have completed a 180-degree turn from coercive power to authority by **influence**. You will take on the role of managing the creative tensions that will lead to progress and development. The tensions, if poorly managed, will turn to conflict. The use of coercive power is like gorging fast food: quick, clean and instantly gratifying but not sustainable or satisfying. By comparison, a joint problem-solving approach is like a quality three-course meal with good wine in good company.

Joint problem-solving requires empowerment, participation, trust and delegation; words that are often paraded to staff in statements of vision, mission, priorities and policies, though there is often a large gap between the preached philosophy and the practice.

These four basic principles are the essential ingredients of cooperation and team building. This does not mean that clear direction is inappropriate. Strong direction is appropriate when an organisation is in serious trouble requiring radical change and there is not sufficient time for participation. It is also appropriate as a part of day-to-day operational management relating to tasks, functions, processes and product that have been clearly outlined and communicated to staff.

There are basic dilemmas faced by all supervisors and managers when considering aspects of empowerment, trust, participation and delegation.

'If I take too much control it implies a lack of trust in those who work for me. On the other hand, the more I empower and involve the staff the more I feel I am giving up control and the harder it is to re-establish it if something goes wrong.'

We would all like those people above us to have a greater degree of trust in us and invite us to be more involved in the real decision making. On the other hand, many of us are reticent to release too much control to those people who report to us. The best managers see their role as identifying, coordinating and developing the collective best of all concerned in the team in a manner which will benefit each participant and the team collectively. These are the managers who will be most effective in conflict situations because they are leading and guiding people rather than merely performing tasks and functions.

Real empowerment, participation and delegation require a higher order of management and supervision. Whereas traditional control is a vertical directive approach, real empowerment requires an approach by which you walk together with the participants. Done well it is more subtle and effective than the coercive directive approach and the improved outcomes will justify the transition.

Put this now in the context of your responsibility as a leader. Think about your involvement in the development of a working environment in which conflict is less likely to occur and the manner in which you will deal with conflict when it does happen. Look now to your own organisation and assess the degree to which it involves the employees in the real workings and decision making. As a guide use the assessment activities in the early part of Chapter 5. Congratulate yourself on the number of high scores and then look to those areas requiring further development.

▶ **Tasks, functions, processes and products do not think, reason, solve problems or make decisions. They do not manage or resolve conflict. People do. So your core responsibility as a supervisor or manager is the effective support, guidance and development of the people who report to you.**

So let us look to best practice in managing people in a manner by which you can more successfully handle conflicts and difficulties. The best managers will progress from the reactive model outlined earlier to a more positive development model.

COOPERATIVE DEVELOPMENT MODEL
In this more positive problem-solving model you:
- Get out and about; move around the staff.
- Are open, honest and transparent with them.
- Listen and hear.
- Look and see.
- Think about and sense what is happening or likely to happen.
- Question and test understanding.
- Research and analyse.
- Anticipate problems before they develop.
- Are strategic in your approach to people's problems.
- Are constructive and developmental.
- Establish preventative strategies.
- Identify and respond to potential issues now (pre-operative).
- Become actively involved in assisting others to achieve resolution and agreement.
- Intervene early as this will be more positive and developmental and will lead to improved outcomes.
- Promote greater job satisfaction.

You might ask: 'When am I going to get time to do all of that when I have all of these important things to do?' If you establish these people matters as your priority you will significantly reduce the time you now spend cleaning up problems and dealing with conflicts and grievances after the event, and you will shift the balance of importance from tasks to people, their development and support.

You might ask the obvious question: 'When I am surrounded by crocodiles how can I focus on the main task of draining the swamp?' I can confidently tell you that, should you not focus on your main role and responsibility of people management, you will always be fighting crocodiles.

A major shift in your style of management will not happen overnight and don't be discouraged when the world does not turn right side up immediately. It takes time, patience, commitment, determination, persistence, courage and confidence. Remember also that such a change will not make conflict go away, because it is inevitable and will continue to occur; but if you adopt this more positive people approach you will be far more effective in dealing with it to the better satisfaction of yourself and others involved.

By so doing you will create an environment in which conflict is less likely to occur. When it does occur, you will be in a position to become involved at an early stage when its management is easier and more likely to have positive outcomes for the disputing parties, yourself and your unit as a whole.

BE YOUR OWN HUMAN RESOURCES MANAGER

Not all organisations have a specialist human resources section or people with the expertise and experience in this area. Where they exist, adopt a joint approach with them when dealing with disputes or difficult situations.

Example

In my early days as a human resources director I tended too much to take on the solving of the people problems of other supervisors and managers. One day, Andrew, an operational manager, asked to sit in on an interview relating to a major conflict. After the meeting I asked Andrew if I could have a copy of the minutes he took of the meeting. He told me that he had not been taking minutes but had been writing advisory notes for himself on how to conduct a difficult interview so that in future he could do it himself. It confirmed in my mind that the highest priority for my role as human resources director should be more as a guidance and support person for others and less on solving their problems for them.

Some time later I mentioned to Andrew that I had few problems passed on from his area. He replied: 'I hope not. I manage my own problems. I will come to you for advice and support but I will only have credibility and respect in my area if I do it myself.'

Admittedly, there are many human resources people who prefer to take over your problems because they believe it enhances their status and relative importance in the organisation. But as a supervisor or manager you should resist the temptation to pass it on to the 'experts'. Use the knowledge, skills and experience of those experts to assist you to deal with the matter yourself. In the early stages and in the most difficult situations you might involve them as part of the team or as a consultant to assist your management of the process, but attempt to hold on to your own agenda and manage the situation yourself.

BENEFITS OF THE JOINT PROBLEM-SOLVING APPROACH

Listed below are some of the obvious benefits of this approach. Note the particular benefits that you believe to be most significant for your area of work, whether it be in the context of you as a supervisor working with those responsible to you, or you working with your colleagues, your supervisor or manager.

- Problem-solving is tackled by using the expertise of the team members collectively.
- A general skills and experience audit of your team will identify an enormous pool of talent, experience and potential that could be better utilised in a team approach. It will also identify those areas requiring further development.
- The process of linking individuals with mentors or guides in the team will enhance the productivity and effectiveness of all.
- The team's goals, priorities and outcomes are established after consideration of the collective contributions of the group.
- Individual goals and expected outcomes are formulated in terms of their participation within the group. This will provide cohesion between the individuals and the unit in which they work.
- All team members, including leaders, are committed to support each other and will work together in difficult situations or when mistakes have been made.
- Members of the team will share resources and their allocation will be flexible to meet changing needs.
- There are clear policies and practices for the professional development of each individual and these are coordinated within a strategic development program for the group.
- Team members are given regular feedback on their performance and this is linked to their training and development.
- Training will include the understanding, awareness and practical application of managing conflict in the workplace. This will be supplemented by training in matters such as anti-discrimination, equal opportunity, sexual harassment, cultural diversity, occupational health and safety, recruitment and selection procedures.
- Individuals, including those with problems, are treated with professional dignity and are given the opportunity to raise issues of concern and have those matters dealt with.
- Everyone understands that conflict, grievances and disagreements are a normal daily occurrence and that they will be acted on as quickly as possible.
- Provision is made for the airing and resolution of grievances and disputes with an emphasis on helping the participants work towards a practical and mutually agreeable resolution to their problem.
- Individuals and the team are given recognition for outstanding work and encouraged to further develop their potential.
- Individuals and groups are encouraged to contribute ideas and to test new strategies.
- There are clear expectations of work and standards to be achieved.
- Each team member understands the responsibilities of others and understands when pressures increase.
- Members will support others as difficulties arise.

- Individuals are willing to relieve other members to assist the team and gain more skills and experience in the process.
- Communication is open, honest and transparent.
- Staff are encouraged and given the opportunity to participate at meetings beyond tokenism.
- There is a healthy balance between the needs and expectations of the individual and those of the team as a whole.
- Working effectively in one team allows individuals to transfer easily to other teams.
- People take pride in the recognition and reward of their group.
- Leaders are members of teams and work with them rather than at them.
- Members are encouraged to manage specific projects and given the necessary support and guidance to do so.
- Effectiveness and outcomes are measured first as a team effort.
- Teamwork and effectiveness go hand in hand.

This is the environment that will reduce the number and intensity of conflicts and place you in a stronger position to deal with it when it occurs. Intuition, lateral thinking and a willingness to test the edges will assist the process.

In the next chapter, we will look at how conflict occurs and develops. We will look to the basic principles underlying the management of conflict in the workplace. This will lead you to identify what must change in order for you to better handle conflict and its resolution.

chapter 2

Understanding conflict

- Basic principles of conflict resolution
- Understanding the differences between ourselves and others
- Power and influence
- Emotion and empathy

■ BASIC PRINCIPLES OF CONFLICT RESOLUTION

As children we were constantly reminded that we should stay away from conflict.

> *'Don't get involved. You might get hurt.'*
> *'It's none of your business. Stay out of it.'*
> *'Let them fight it out by themselves.'*
> *'It's their fault. They can sort it out.'*
> *'Stay away from those horrible people. Don't have anything to do with them.'*

There are some basic principles that underlie the management of conflict in the workplace.

- The first priority is to create a working environment in which conflict is least likely to occur. This preventative approach focuses on recognising and enhancing the positive attributes of each individual and the development of a cooperative, cohesive and empowered team. The obvious benefits are improved morale, job satisfaction, productivity, reduced costs and fewer disruptions.
- Relationships are open and honest, and individuals have access to information, training, guidance and job opportunities.
- Effective policies, procedures and strategies are established and communicated clearly to the staff through positive development programs:
- Management walks with the staff instead of at them to ensure that employees have a sense of ownership of their programs.
- Management is in a position to anticipate and deal with problems before they develop.
- When conflict does occur it is dealt with it quickly before it develops further.
- In the first instance, conflict is dealt with informally, with time and space given to establish the facts and clear away irrelevant matters.
- The prime objective is an agreed resolution with a commitment from all concerned to a common course of action.

As a leader you can no longer avoid being involved in disputes and their resolution. Your ability to handle these matters is one of the most important aspects of your work. Be clear in identifying your roles and responsibilities, including the most important role of people management and development. Be certain that all staff members understand their responsibilities and how you want them to interact with and relate to you. Provide clear guidelines, policies and procedures to all members of staff. Plan for the management of grievances and establish mechanisms for handling disputes.

Be a leader in dispute resolution. Make it happen, don't sit back and wait for someone to take over. Hold on to your own agenda or you will find that you will be always reacting and dancing to someone else's tune. The moment you step aside from that major responsibility you leave a vacuum which will be filled by someone else; most likely one of the disputants. At that stage you no longer have control: they do. Be in the position whereby you are putting the options on the table for others to consider or where you are the one assisting others to mould the combined thinking of the group towards an agreed agenda. They will then be reacting to your proposals.

Question, listen, hear, clarify and analyse on a daily basis so that you know what is going on. Be in a position where you can anticipate most of the problems before they happen or, at worst, be in a position where you can take action in the early stages of a dispute. Supplement this with the provision of advice, guidance, mentoring, support and development to meet the needs of your staff. The most powerful influence you can exert in any organisation is your ability to develop other staff members.

Do not make assumptions about people or situations and then look for the evidence to justify that assumption. Clarify the factual evidence first and then base your decisions or guidance on that. Understand your emotions. Try to understand the intricacies of office politics and how they impact on people's performance. Enhance your communication skills and learn to read and understand your behaviour as well as the behaviour of others. Deal with negative behaviour as it arises, not after it has developed into a crisis. Establish procedures that lead to the early identification of problem situations and early intervention. This will allow you to actively establish a preventative mode of operation instead of taking a reactive stance to everyone else.

BENEFITS OF A POSITIVE APPROACH

By developing a positive preventative approach to people management, it is more likely that problem-solving and dispute resolution will be tackled by using the expertise of the team members collectively. Individual staff members will be more likely to become involved in team activities when they know that their concerns are being addressed quickly, fairly, openly and honestly. This will create an environment in which team members are more likely to contribute to the collective goals, priorities and outcomes of the group and in which they will develop more respect for other members of staff and for you as their leader.

When mistakes are made or problems occur the team is more likely to work together to solve them, rather than retreat into a cloud of negative criticism leaving it to someone else to fix. Everyone is recognised for their level of skill, experience and contribution and is committed to support each other knowing that their efforts are being rewarded, their potential is being developed and their ideas are being considered.

Staff will support each other as difficulties arise and be more willing to be flexible in their work practices to meet fluctuations in work demands. A healthy balance between the needs and expectations of the individual and those of the group and the organisation will develop over time, and as people gain more confidence in themselves, others and you, this will accelerate.

WHAT ARE WE AIMING FOR?

In trying to resolve conflicts and deal with difficult situations there has always been an obsession about gaining a win–win result which appears to most of us in the workplace as an unreal expectation. Most of the literature will discuss lose–lose, win–lose and win–win situations, and will lead you towards the ideal of a win–win. I find the examples used in the literature bear too little resemblance to real life in the workplace.

How realistic is it to your work situation? How many times have you been involved in a major conflict or have observed other conflicts in which both parties have walked away believing that they have had a win? Striving for a win–win resolution in the real world produces unreal expectations in the minds of the conflicting parties and the supervisor who has to manage the process. Real conflicts come with a lot of anger, emotion and stress with resulting physical, emotional or psychological damage. In those situations the parties are more likely to avoid dealing with the matter rather than expend a lot of emotional energy on something that they perceive as unachievable.

Too often one person walks away in order to relieve the continuing stress and will agree to anything in order to have peace and quiet. They see the release of tension that comes with a walkout as a win because the alternative of continuing the rage will be more destructive. 'Do whatever you like but just leave me alone.' In these situations the matter is rarely solved or settled. It is merely delayed and will emerge again at a later date in this or another format. We have to be more realistic.

The best operators in handling difficult situations between conflicting parties strive to achieve **resolution** by commitment to an **agreed** action through a combined effort of **problem-solving**.

> ► The emphasis has to be on achieving agreement. It does not require a feeling of win–win. It does not require the parties to love or even like each other, or to like you as the manager of the situation. Hopefully, if you have achieved agreement, there will be a respect for the manner by which you handled the process. If you can achieve that, then the likelihood of resolution the next time improves, and your employees will gradually see you as someone who is open, honest and fair and in whom they have trust and confidence. This in turn will have a multiplier effect on all other areas of the workplace and management.

Consider the following points:
- When both parties agree to a resolution there is a greater commitment by both sides to the outcomes of that agreement.
- For that to happen something, or someone, must change.
- The first thing to change is your approach to dealing with and managing disputes.
- The implementation of the agreement must be monitored.

- Because they are in a dispute situation assume that the parties lack some vital knowledge, skills, experience and the inability to handle difficult situations.
- Guidance, support and development is required by the parties to assist them to manage the agreement.

COMMITMENT TO MANAGING YOUR HUMAN RESOURCES RESPONSIBILITIES

There are many people in supervisory or managerial positions who do not want or like to be involved in people issues, problems and disputes. These people are reticent to act because they might not like admitting their mistakes: they feel an exposure of their shortcomings will lessen their power and influence and see disputes as problems that might reflect on their career prospects. They want a perfect solution before they become involved because they always want to be seen as right. They see compromise as a weakness and a loss of territory or possessions. These people have difficulty apologising and feel uncomfortable bargaining or negotiating; they are ill at ease dealing with the ambiguity and inconsistency of human behaviour.

Many people do not have the knowledge, skills, awareness, understanding, training, guidance and experience to handle conflict management. They have difficulty separating the people from the problem or not taking sides. This significantly reduces their courage and confidence to take risks or to handle a crisis when it occurs.

Instead of passing your people problems to the human resources unit, use them or other people for whom you have respect, as a source of information, a pool of ideas and strategies, an avenue of support for guidance and training and as a back-up of expertise when required. With these resources available in the background the best operators take on the responsibility for their own human resources.

Watch the best leaders move in quickly, take charge of the situation, clarify the issues, set the agenda for resolution and get on with the job of assisting others come to an agreement through a joint problem-solving approach. Compare it with those who avoid the difficulty or become too emotionally involved, or those who mishandle its management. Compare it also with those who pass the problem to someone else and then complain about the manner in which it was handled.

The best leaders will project their courage, ability, trust and experience into the arena. They accept their strengths and limitations but have the confidence to take control of the matter when everyone else is losing their sense of control. These are the people who are willing to assist others in dealing with disputes. They will:
- assess their involvement in the situation;
- be willing to identify their own gaps or mistakes;
- assess their approach and determine whether it is inflaming or calming;
- manage their own emotions and feelings first;
- try to reduce or remove the log jams, hurdles, fires and mud;
- question others and listen to their responses;

- clarify the issues;
- assess the need for support or information;
- discuss the approaches with the others;
- manage the process of resolution.

For you to be truly effective you will want to be involved in dispute resolution and management because the alternative is not an option. To move from a stance of negative avoidance to one of positive management it is best to observe the top operators in action and ask to be present when they are handling major disputes. Then seek advice from the experts, research this area, review your policies and procedures and seek the involvement of your staff in developing new guidelines to be used when disputes and grievances occur.

■ CONFLICT IS A DYSFUNCTION OF COMMUNICATION

Dysfunction or friction within groups can very often be traced back to breakdowns in communication. If we neglect to speak and hear precisely, our understanding will always be flawed.

UNDERSTAND?
I know you believe that you understand
that which you think I said;
but I am not sure you realise that,
what you thought I said
was not really what I understand
that which I believe
I really meant to say.
If you know what I mean.

'It's on the top shelf of the cupboard.'
'No it's not. I can't find it there. It must be somewhere else.'
'Open your eyes stupid. Look again. I know I put it there this morning. You can't trust
*   anyone these days to do the most simple thing.'*
'I have looked twice. It is NOT there.'
'There it is; exactly where I said it was; on the top shelf. Get yourself a seeing-eye
*   dog, stupid. You are so hopeless.'*
'But that's not the cupboard where you normally keep it.'
'Yes it is. I changed it over when I tidied up last week. You were there when I did it.'

It is important to:
- look and see
- question and analyse
- listen and hear
- think and understand.

Whenever I have acted as a mediator, or have been asked to be involved with difficult negotiations, or have been asked to assist with dysfunctional units, there has always been an underlying cause of faulty communication. Other factors might or might not be present but you can guarantee that poor communication will always be a factor. In some cases it has reached a state where there is no further communication between the conflicting parties and the situation becomes a remote Mexican stand-off. When communications break down there is no way that the organisation can continue to be functional and effective. In other cases, conflict could result from the withholding or the selective release of information, poor expression, language barriers, inability or disinclination to listen, or a distortion of the communication along the line.

You can only deal with conflict by addressing the problems of communication between the combatants and this goes well beyond what was said directly between them. It is important to search out the original source of the message and the context in which it was transmitted. For example, you might be having a dispute with a colleague about a policy or message that came originally from the chief general manager. Test first that your colleague has passed on the correct message. The same person will transmit differences in the message in different circumstances. What the chief says to your colleague at the golf club over a few drinks might be quite different from what he or she will say at a formal staff meeting.

In simple terms, communication is the transmission of a message from one person to another person or group. But that communication can be distorted at the source, at various stages in the transmission or by the receiver. These distortions are a major factor of the causes and development of conflict.

Example
Consider the impact someone like Cassius the Backstabber can have on an organisation. He is a schemer who rarely confronts you directly. He likes to talk about you behind your back and will be seen in small groups muttering negative comments about others confidentially behind his hand. He picks up and exaggerates the anxieties of others and makes it appear that he is supportive when, in fact, he is using this as ammunition to denigrate them to others and others to them.

He loves using suggestion and innuendo to create an image of concern and will seek others' support before he strikes. He will say complimentary things to others while criticising you and often pretends to be innocent. He will load the gun but often gets another to pull the trigger.

Look to the activities in Chapter 5 regarding problems in communication over the transmission of the message, the distortions that occur along the way and difficulties with the receiver. Relate these to your own experience and the workplace in which you operate. Put all of these matters in the context of conflicts in which you have been involved or which you have witnessed and assess the extent to which these issues played a significant part in the commencement, development and resolution of the conflict. Look then to the manner in which you will overcome these problems and improve communication to reach agreement and resolution.

The best leaders of conflict management are those who have developed excellent skills of questioning and listening and use them to good effect to tease out the facts and explore options. They constantly feed back information and viewpoints to test their understanding of what others have said, and use a range of questions to search for the detail. They also invite cooperation from others by promoting the feeling that the other person's views are valued and will be taken into consideration in determining the outcomes. These leaders create a positive environment in which to conduct interviews — one which encourages people to be open, forthright and honest.

Example
Consider an interview with someone like Aggro Andy. He is a time bomb waiting to explode. He shouts and screams, has aggressive body language with intense displays of verbal abuse. He likes to confront head on with exaggerated tantrums and he constantly inflames the issue. He is forceful, high-pressure and intense, highly emotional, negative and destructive. He attacks the person, and not the issue or problem, and ignores other opinions or tries to destroy them. He has learnt by experience that displays of anger make others avoid him and so he lets anger hide his inadequacies.

I have found that the best approach to dealing with Andy is to invite him to express his concerns while assuring him that you will investigate the matters raised. While he is venting his spleen, take notes and when he has run out of steam read back what he has said to test that you have an accurate record of his concerns. Follow this with some astute questioning to bring out the facts and necessary detail. 'What? Who? When? Where?' Then investigate those concerns. When you are convinced that you have all the facts, have another interview to feed back your findings to him.

■ UNDERSTANDING THE DIFFERENCES BETWEEN OURSELVES AND OTHERS

In Chapter 1, I stated that most conflict occurs because people are different and not necessarily because they are wrong. So, our first priority as managers is to understand the concept of diversity and difference and how that leads to a development of a conflict situation. In turn, we might then apply our skills, knowledge, awareness, understanding and experience to better manage those differences and the situations in which they operate together. We need to understand how conflict develops and how it impacts on people in the workplace.

The increased flow of people across countries, the constant change by organisations worldwide, and the drive for economic advantage has led, over the last 20 years or so, to substantial changes in the demographics of the workplace. This in turn has exaggerated the differences that you must address.

Conflict resolution and its management, therefore, is a matter of altering the status quo or changing the balance between competing forces. One or more sides will be trying to advance their proposals for change while the others will be trying to maintain the status quo in order to maintain their comparative advantage. It is a very competitive world and will continue to be so. Just think of the ways you are competitive in the workplace. Do you try to establish an advantage over your colleagues? Has that led to clashes and disputes?

The obvious starting point is to look to the different ways we operate as supervisors and managers; our leadership style; how we try to get across our messages and how we relate to those for whom we have responsibility.

DIFFERENT STYLES OF OPERATION

There are a number of different programs available to assess your competency or style as a manager. These include the Myers-Briggs Type Indicator, Disk, Marc Management Competency Profile, Firo B and Seven Dimensions. Most of these tools can be self-administered or used across the organisation as a part of a total analysis.

The model that I have developed is easy to use and very flexible. It does not lock you down with labels or put you permanently into boxes. It allows for changing circumstances at work and over time throughout your development. It is not a static model. No model is perfect and will not give all the answers; so it should be used, like all other such tools, as a general indicator in conjunction with other measuring strategies. Because humans act differently in different circumstances, times and places these tools can only be used as a broad indicator of your operational style and behaviour and should not be set as an absolute concrete image.

Ask your staff, colleagues and your superior to assess you using the same instrument. This 360-degree exercise will give you a better understanding of how you are seen by others and, in turn, this will allow you to reassess the manner in which you relate to others, especially in difficult situations. It will reveal aspects of you that were not obvious to you beforehand.

I want you now to look to the factors listed in the four segments of the model on the following pages (Figure 2.1) and tick each one that you believe to be one of your strong characteristics or to reflect the manner in which you normally operate. Tick those factors that you perceive as genuine aspects of you. Do not tick merely because it is the way you would like others to view your operation. When you have finished, count the number of ticks in each of the four segments.

There is no prize for the highest number of ticks.

FIGURE 2.1
The Dicker Model of operational style or mode

SEGMENT A		SEGMENT B	
Concentrates easily	☐	Creates harmony	☐
Conservative	☐	Deep sensitivity	☐
Conscientious	☐	Praises rather than criticises	☐
Restrained approach	☐	Stable, secure	☐
Always ready on time	☐	Loves peace and quiet	☐
Gives priority to detail and organisation	☐	Strongly loyal	☐
Demands excellence	☐	Rarely jumps to conclusions	☐
Steady and sure	☐	Likes helping others	☐
Enjoys research and analysis	☐	Quiet manner	☐
Judgmental	☐	Cautious until clearly convinced	☐
Methodical	☐	Difficulty saying no	☐
Must have clear guidelines	☐	Values cooperation over competition	☐
Meticulous, thorough	☐	Likes to be liked	☐
Very orderly	☐	Tendency to procrastinate	☐
Task-oriented	☐	Likes to show commitment	☐
Demands accuracy	☐	Calming influence	☐
Decisions based on facts	☐	Listens attentively	☐
Likes rules, regulations, procedures	☐	Prefers others to lead	☐
Careful in planning	☐	Secure, long-term relationships	☐
Responsible	☐	Compassionate	☐
Industrious	☐	Prefers slow, controlled change	☐
Values what we have	☐	Expresses values	☐
Practical	☐	Let's think about it carefully	☐

© Laurie Dicker

SEGMENT C	
Persuasive	☐
Forceful	☐
Pragmatic	☐
Pushes for tangible results	☐
Likes a challenge	☐
Clear personal goals	☐
Willing to confront	☐
Very direct	☐
Makes decisions easily	☐
Keen to test it	☐
Gets bored with details	☐
Likes to progress	☐
Has a sense of urgency	☐
Likes clearing obstacles	☐
Acts with authority	☐
Handles crises	☐
Likes to lead	☐
Enjoys solving problems	☐
Brings about change	☐
Resourceful	☐
Let's do it	☐
Deals easily with the unexpected	☐
Action person	☐

SEGMENT D	
Interactive	☐
Outgoing	☐
Informal	☐
Likes friendly and open environment	☐
Expressive communication	☐
Energetic and active	☐
Intuitive	☐
Emphasises enjoyment	☐
Creative	☐
Flamboyant	☐
Prefers broad approach	☐
Likes working in groups	☐
Creates motivational environment	☐
Expresses emotions	☐
Often acts on impulse	☐
Willing to express feelings	☐
Enjoys discussing options	☐
Likes a changing environment	☐
Innovative	☐
Flexible	☐
Risk taker	☐
Visionary	☐
Let's change it	☐

Do not put yourself into neat little pigeon holes!

We are human beings, not physical structures. We are flexible and changeable and while we might display a general pattern of behaviour, there is quite a deal of variation within that pattern. It is what makes people management the most interesting aspect of your responsibility as a leader. It will also cause you the most headaches if you don't get it right, because people don't always follow the rules and prescribed patterns as does a piece of machinery. The exercise of putting ticks in each segment is only the preliminary exercise. Now follow the seven steps.

STEP 1: LOOK TO YOUR STRENGTHS IN EACH SEGMENT
Am I a traditional well-organised person from Segment A?
People who have most ticks in this segment are usually more ordered in their life; systematic; disciplined and they proceed by the law, policy, guidelines and regulations. They are very strong on detailed correctness and fit comfortably into roles associated with administration, coordination, financial management and construction. They are strongly focused on task, function, process and product. They usually focus more on efficiency and output than effectiveness and outcomes.

They are recognised by others for their great value in maintaining good order and discipline in the organisation and bringing order out of chaos, but they are often seen by others as boring, pedantic, nit-picking and too hide-bound by petty rules and regulations. These are not necessarily faults as they are a necessary component of a good organisation, but they irritate others and so are potential issues for conflict.

Do I lean strongly to a people focus in Segment B?
People strong in this segment are more inclined to desire a secure, stable, working environment and do not like change. They are usually very dedicated, loyal, hard working, enthusiastic workers who like to be told what to do and then left to get on with it uninterrupted. They are sensitive to others in the group and will provide the necessary emotional and compassionate support to those in trouble, but they do not like dealing with the difficult crises and do not adapt easily to change. They have strong attributes in the people business. They have good personal qualities and strong interpersonal relationships.

Organisations realise that these are the dependable people who get the work done and who are very valuable to the team; but they are sometimes seen by others as soft, over-caring wimps who get too distracted by emotional issues.

Am I an active, dominant, leader type from Segment C?
Dominance in this segment reflects a person who is very directive; someone who wants to take the lead and wield the power. They are not afraid to take risks and make decisions. They are action people. They work well as project managers where they can bring together a wide range of physical and human resources to achieve positive outcomes

in a new area of endeavour. They like taking an organisation through a change process but are less comfortable in a stable or consolidating environment.

Despite these good qualities, others sometimes see them as too dominant, bossy, arrogant and intolerant of the needs of other people.

Am I a creative visionary from Segment D?

Strength in this segment reflects a person who is creative, visionary, flamboyant, usually talkative and expressive. They are the people who look to the sky and the horizon while others count the grains of sand or contemplate the fluff in their navel. They enjoy social events and will party until they drop. They show strength in planning and development, public relations and presentations. They are more inclined towards intuitive thinking rather than practical doing. They provide a very good balance in a team to Segment A people.

Others sometimes see these people as unreliable, off with the fairies, disorganised, too disruptive, too talkative and enjoying life too much to be dependable workers.

STEP 2: HOW BALANCED ARE YOU ACROSS THE FOUR SEGMENTS?

Nobody is totally in one segment. Many of us have a reasonably even balance of ticks in all segments, and therefore have the potential to be good negotiators or mediators because we can see issues from all sides and thus can assist disputing parties to walk together towards agreement and resolution.

Look to your own balance. Where are your strengths? In which areas do you depend on other people to meet your shortfall? In what areas should you consider further development to enhance a shortfall? For example, should people from Segment D consider doing courses in budgeting and financial management in order to acheive a better understanding and perspective of those processes?

STEP 3: HOW DO YOU CREATE THE BEST TEAMS?

The best teams and, therefore, the ones in which conflict is better managed are those that have a combination of different people from different backgrounds so that each complements the others and adds to their qualities and strengths. The main difficulty for you is to manage and coordinate those differences in a manner in which all parties will make significant contributions to the team. Aim for a cohesion where those contributions are valued by all concerned, where the total is more than the sum of the parts, and where the different skills and experiences will be combined as a cooperative strength.

STEP 4: HOW WILL WE CHANGE OVER TIME?

Nobody is exactly the same throughout one's working life. People mature and develop as they are influenced by others or different circumstances. Each of us has a hidden potential that will gradually emerge as we mature. We will often make significant changes in direction following those experiences and the emergence of our potential. Maturity is an important factor in that change.

When I started work I had a dominance in Segment B and was content to remain there. As I took on more responsibility my latent potential in Segment C emerged; that was followed later by the emergence of my creative and planning qualities from Segment D. Though I have a number of ticks in Segment A, it is not my dominant area. Had you told me early in my career that I would eventually become a specialist in human resources, crisis management and industrial relations, I would have called the men in the white coats to take you away. My changes in direction came as my interests changed and after I experienced different responsibilities that helped to develop my latent potential.

STEP 5: WHAT IS MY POTENTIAL?

This model does not indicate your untapped potential. For most people more than 60 per cent of their potential has not yet been utilised because they have not put themselves in a position to bring out that potential. For most of us it is more comfortable to remain where we are, even when that causes frustration, anger and potential conflict. When you have not been in a position to test the edges and push the boundaries into the unknown, it can be a terrifying prospect. For others who follow their dreams, take the risks and grab the opportunities, the latent potential will emerge.

Try to look for indicators of an untapped potential. Look particularly at areas of your strong interests that might not yet be fulfilled. I recently saw a statement on a T-shirt: 'If you are not living at the edge you are taking up too much space.'

Your role as a supervisor or manager is to develop the potential of your staff by placing them in situations that encourages potential to emerge. Suppressed potential is a recipe for frustration and conflict.

STEP 6: UTILISE YOUR STRENGTHS ACCORDING TO THE SITUATION

If you recognise your strengths in each of the segments you can call upon any of these to meet particular circumstances. If you are dealing with someone who has a terminal illness you will draw upon strengths from Segment B: sensitivity, compassion and helping skills. In preparing a budget or strategic plan then Segment A and Segment D qualities would be helpful. If you have to suddenly bring together different groups to deal with a major crisis then use the strengths of Segment C. If preparing a new dynamic advertising campaign utilise the creativity and planning of Segment D.

In the real world you will use a combination of strengths to best handle difficult situations and conflicts. This will be easier if you know the strengths upon which you can depend.

STEP 7: DIFFERENCES HAVE THE POTENTIAL FOR CONFLICT

On a personal level and in the workplace most conflicts occur because of differences rather than fault. In a group situation the person most likely to conflict with others is the one who shows extremes towards one style of operation. This would be shown on our model as a very high number of ticks in one segment and few in the other three and especially in the opposite segment. These are the people who have the least understanding or tolerance towards others. The people least likely to cause conflict and best able to manage it are the ones with an even balance over the four segments. These people are good negotiators and mediators because they can understand the direction from which each person comes.

WHAT ARE THE IMPLICATIONS FOR YOU?

Having worked through this exercise you need now to look for indicators that will point you in the direction of your strengths, or clarify areas for which you will require further development in order to improve your management style and your ability to manage difficult situations.

■ POWER AND INFLUENCE

Power, authority, influence and assertiveness are important factors in the development of conflict situations and in the means by which agreement and resolution are attained. But the terms are often confused and misused. Look to the meanings below and then assess how you go about changing other people's thinking or actions. Assess the appropriateness of your current style and where there is a need for improvement.

POWER

Power is the ability of one person or group to modify the thoughts or actions of another person or group. Too often we think of power in terms of great physical strength or aggressive coercion and these images tend to have negative or positive overtones depending on whether you are the recipient or the giver of that power. But every organisation requires someone to take control, make decisions and ensure that actions are carried out for the benefit of the organisation and everyone associated with it.

In fact, power can be quite subtle and positive. Those who always have to depend on a pit bull terrier approach to power have very little else to offer in the realm of modern leadership.

People who use dominant power plays will usually be trying to manipulate or pervert the process to gain a distinct advantage for themselves, usually to the disadvantage of the other party. The other person is given few options and is pushed into accepting or fighting the power play.

On the other hand, those with positive personal power will use it to gain cooperation and cohesion, rather than to create fear and antagonism.

AUTHORITY

Authority exists when power is recognised legitimately and so has some official status. Remember, however, that the official status, position, titles, badges, brass and epaulettes might give you authority and the trappings of power, but do not in themselves give you the ability to influence.

In my earlier days I was a football referee and I came to realise very quickly that, when 10 000 people in unison were questioning my parents' relationship and using words that I could not find in the dictionary or thesaurus, the title, badge and whistle did nothing to earn me any respect. It might have given me power and authority but the respect had to be earned by my ability to manage the differences between the players and the conflicts that occurred on the field.

INFLUENCE

Influence is defined in the *Oxford Dictionary* as the action of a person upon another, perceptible only in its effects. It is synonymous with power but is used to refer to a more subtle use of that power. In that way it is seen as less overt, aggressive and coercive. It is a form of power that is more likely to invite and encourage cooperation, cohesion, collaboration and participation.

The best operators look to gaining the most for all parties and the group rather than themselves. They will put the options on the table but will be willing to listen to the other person's response and their alternative suggestions. Under these circumstances the other person has more chance to make a choice in an open, honest and transparent atmosphere.

In the real world, people using this approach may manipulate and control others, but they will be more open about it. They will use their greater intellect, their more careful research and analysis, their better knowledge and understanding, experience, ability to formulate options, personal persuasiveness and charisma to lead the others to their way of thinking or towards a preferred agreed action. This form of manipulation is a more subtle form than aggression or coercion in its application.

ASSERTIVENESS

Assertiveness is the right and ability to state one's case, to have and to put forward an opinion, to establish a claim and have it heard, to make a positive statement or to make a declaration.Unfortunately, many people mistake aggression for assertiveness, and they use coercion to get their point of view across.

The most influential assertiveness is marked by a calm, controlled and confident presentation pitched at the perceptive level of the audience who will, in response, have little difficulty in understanding what you want to say and to respect your views and opinions.

EMPOWERMENT

Empowerment is a situation, a state of mind or a happening in which you are free to make real decisions about yourself and in which you are enabled to make real contributions to the matter at hand. The underlying principle to this concept is a freedom of choice. If empowered you have been endowed with the authority to be involved in your own destiny that, in turn, will give you the confidence, energy, drive and moral strength to get involved. While involvement carries with it responsibility, it will at least give you the reward of knowing that you have something of value to contribute.

Empowerment in the workplace means the establishment of equality in relationships, equity of opportunity and an open access to information and resources. It is essential to any concept of joint participation in problem-solving. People who feel and act empowered have a high energy and enthusiasm, will look for opportunities for growth and development, and focus on the positives in any situation. These people learn from their mistakes and will concentrate on the now and the future rather than dwell on the disasters of the past. They are the people who attempt to establish their influence in conjunction with other people, rather than use power against them. They are more confident in walking with the other person towards a positive agreement and resolution. They accept life as it is and then get on with trying to improve it.

Power, authority, influence, assertiveness and empowerment make up the fine interconnecting web joining individuals, groups, communities and organisations. They are the processes by which one person can modify the behaviour of another person or group. Each organisation is made up of people, singly or collectively, trying to influence others to think and act in a certain way.

Each person, unless totally isolated from humanity, will form psychological contact with a number of individuals and groups as in families, at work, in sport, social groups, community associations, political organisations or with friends.

In assessing your role within those groups, ask yourself a number of questions:
- To what extent do I wish to maintain my individuality?
- How much freedom do I wish to have?
- How much freedom am I willing to give up?
- In what areas am I willing to give up my freedom?
- In what areas will I try to maintain control?
- Whom do I respect to give me guidance?
- Who could I influence, guide, support or mentor?
- What are the limits of my toleration?
- How can I seek out the influences I desire?
- How do I stop unwanted influence?

Example
Conflict is often caused when one person wishes to dominate others by the overt use of power. There is often a Dictator Dan in an organisation. He likes to put you down

and belittle you. He is a dictator, autocrat, bully and a bulldozer who rules from a position of power. Any suggested change is a threat to his authority and is taken as an implied criticism. He gets angry very quickly; is often aggressive and usually loud, demands loyalty without question. There is only one god and he will kill off those not considered totally loyal and obedient. He is fast to attack; catches you off guard; acts quickly and causes injury with little compassion and sensitivity. He adopts an 'I win you lose' attitude and you will always lose because he has a desperate desire for power and control and his greatest fear is the loss of that power and status.

Avoid confronting Dan in public because he likes an audience when he goes in for a kill. Do your homework, be well prepared and give him recognition for his position and status by massaging his ego. It is important to give him time and space to consider any proposal because any request for an immediate answer will result in rejection and ridicule. Keep asking questions to show that you are on top of the matter being discussed. Remain calm and in control of your emotions. When he sees that he cannot dominate you he will look for another wimp on whom to vent his spleen. It takes confidence and courage and this will only come with good preparation.

FUNDAMENTALS OF BEHAVIOUR

In dealing with individuals and groups be guided by some basic principles of human behaviour as it applies in the workplace. This is not an exhaustive list and I invite you to add to it from your own experience.

- People appreciate group work but need individual recognition.
- People have a strong motivation of self-interest.
- They like to do things for their reasons, not yours.
- They want the opportunity to be listened to and heard.
- They have different needs, expectations, fears, values and styles of operation.
- They react differently to crisis situations.
- They act differently to the same type of crisis in different circumstances.
- Most people appreciate honest feedback that is supported by clear factual evidence.
- Most people will avoid difficult situations for as long as possible.
- Most people prefer to be advised rather than told.
- They will accept decisions that are well founded and clearly stated.
- They appreciate positive support and guidance.
- They are motivated by real opportunities to achieve success.
- Their interests change and are not always clearly stated.
- Staff will be more willing to carry out work they helped to design.
- There is always an element of emotion and stress in disputes.
- People instinctively take up positions to reduce their uncertainty.
- They will attempt to protect what they believe is theirs.

- People appreciate time and space to consider options.
- They appreciate recognition and reward.
- It is easier to deal with people who respect you.
- Their respect must be earned, not demanded.
- People do not have to like or love you, or even agree with you to have respect for you.
- They will devise games and strategies to distract or weaken your position.

DEVELOPMENT OF A CONFLICT

Conflicts, if allowed to, will develop progressively from a mild irritation to a major outburst or explosion where serious damage can be done. Because most people tend to avoid dealing with the conflict or grievance in the early stages it is allowed to develop to a stage where they have to address negative, destructive actions and pressures and then adopt a reactive stance to its management. If ignored or avoided a conflict will progress through a number of stages.

Irritation

In the earliest stages a difference between two people will appear as a minor irritation. It could be as simple as leaving a dirty coffee cup on your table or failing to put back a piece of borrowed equipment. A male supervisor stands too close to a young female staff member. When it happens for the first time it is more in the context of a minor irritation.

At this early stage most people tend to ignore it or brush it lightly aside. They might feel uncomfortable but generally are not inclined to act because they see that to take action will increase the pressure on themselves and this they could do well without.

Discomfort

If left, the difference will develop further, with one or both sides taking more liberties. Individual actions will now cause annoyance and concern. Again, most people will walk away or try to make a joke about it in an attempt to lessen the impact. The coffee cup left stains on the table and on some papers. The tools were returned blunt. The supervisor tends to stand at the woman's desk in such a manner that he can see down the front of her dress.

Hurt

As the differences become magnified, the actions and reactions become more intense and as a result someone will be genuinely stressed by the incident. The other person sits with their feet on your table, the coffee is spilt on a document you were to hand to the chief this morning. Your tools were returned with a chip out of one blade. The supervisor is inclined to give the staff member a hug every now and then.

In these circumstances the victim might scowl, frown and posture with their body language but will still be disinclined to act directly if they see the other person as more powerful. They are also disinclined to take action if the other person is their supervisor or superior.

Pain

At this stage there is an obvious inflammation of the conflict. The other person moves all of your material off your desk so that there is ample space to put their feet, lunch, coffee, cake or their smelly sneakers after their lunchtime run. The other person lends your tools to someone else but does not know where they are now. The supervisor has taken to squeezing the young staff member's bottom and showing her suggestive pictures he has downloaded from the Internet. There is genuine anger, resentment and stress in these cases.

Those who don't deal with it directly are more likely to express their feelings and work out their frustration with friends and colleagues to gain comfort and support from their warm comments and agreements. But this in itself will not solve the problems. If it is not addressed, the problem will progress further.

Agony

This is a situation that causes severe pain, extreme tension and much stress and it will seriously affect one's well-being. Other members of staff become involved and there are obvious divisions according to loyalties to one side or the other. There is extreme hurt, anger, enmity, bitterness and contempt. Much of this is expressed in exaggerated body language; but if the real causes are not addressed a major conflict will occur. The person has taken confidential papers from your desk and lost them. The person who has your tools has left the company and taken your tools with them. The supervisor has driven the staff member to a training day, after which he has taken her to a club for drinks and on the way home he demands to have sex.

Eruption

In a conflict situation there is a loss of control, anger, fighting, bitterness and extreme stress and sickness. At this stage it is difficult to retrieve the situation and restore relationships to their original manageable positions. Too often managers enter at this point to 'fix' it by transferring staff because they are having a 'personality clash' or 'can't get on with each other'.

What would you do to address these issues if they were taking place among your staff?

The first step is to break into the pattern as quickly as possible and to deal with the issues in the early stages. It is then easy to manage: the people are willing to be involved in coming to a resolution of the problem with the least disruption and maximum cooperation. At this stage it is also more likely that the process of problem-solving will look for positive options instead of expending valuable time and energy on the negative and destructive emotions and attacks.

To assist this early intervention it is important to read the signs that indicate a potential or real conflict. Look and see, listen and hear, think and understand what is going on. But you can't do that from a closed office, communicating only by email.

REACTIONS TO POWER AND CONFLICT

As I have said, most people are not comfortable or confident in dealing with conflict. They see it as an unnecessary interruption or distraction from what they want or need to do; what they perceive as the important issues of the day; tasks, functions, processes or products that clearly fit into their area of responsibility. They see also that involvement in handling conflict is too stressful and so they will avoid it at all costs. Because of this avoidance, conflict will often develop further.

Others deal with conflict through aggression because it appeals to them as the quickest and easiest solution. They gain some satisfaction from their overt display of power and authority to 'cure' it. It establishes for them, and they hope for others, a recognition of their control and territory. From your experience think of those at your workplace who bark, bite and symbolically mark their territorial corner posts to establish their power, authority and status. How many of these people effectively resolve conflict, reach agreement on critical issues or create a better working environment in which people have trust and confidence? Recognise that these people might achieve a quick solution to a perceived problem at a relatively low cost in the short term, but what are the long-term costs in relation to cooperation, collaboration, contribution, cohesion and teamwork? Look to the levels of sick leave, resignation rates, backlogs, product returns, grievances and industrial activity in that workplace.

As someone responsible for the supervision or management of people, you can no longer avoid being directly involved in conflict resolution or dealing with difficult situations. In the 21st century it is no longer possible for you and others to continue to get ahead merely on the quality of your technical and professional skills. Your success as a leader will depend on your people skills. This will include your ability to analyse and understand those with whom you associate; your effective communication with them; your recognition of their differences; your skill in handling their tensions and grievances; the manner in which you address their critical needs and concerns; and your involvement in their professional growth and development.

The changing working environment in which more work is being done by fewer people is creating more frustration, physical and mental tiredness, backlogs, changed procedures and limited training and development. This is the environment in which interpersonal conflict is more likely to occur. As I have said a number of times already, your most important skills will relate to people management; your ability to guide, mentor, influence, inspire, develop and motivate the people who report to you and to mould their differences into an effective team. To gain their cooperation you must be seen to listen to and respond to their needs, concerns and differences and then guide them to resolution and agreement of their conflicts. Delegate the tasks and then manage the people. People management will become the key focus of successful management because, without it, there will be little else to sustain the organisation.

■ UNDERSTANDING EMOTION AND EMPATHY

To cultivate effective people skills you will need some insight into the emotional response of others and an ability to empathise without surrendering.

EMOTION

Conflicts always contain some element of emotion that might range from mild tension to full-blown aggression. Because emotion is potentially stressful, most people will try to avoid it. Our emotions can be so powerful that they can have a negative impact on us and make it difficult to focus on the priorities at hand. Most of us are aware of the impact that grief has on our well-being in times of a loss of a close friend or loved one, and how that affects our ability to think and act clearly. Some of us can suppress the overt emotion associated with grief for some time and appear to be unaffected by the loss; but it is better for us to release the tension and allow the grief to emerge. While I would not suggest that you let go of all control to the point that you abuse and upset people around you, it is advisable to find some release for your tensions.

Unfortunately, as children most of us, and especially boys, were taught to control or suppress our emotions. We were expected to be stoic and control our passions, our fears and even our pleasures. It was considered a weakness if a boy cried. Those who promoted these ideals failed to realise the impact of pent-up emotions on the mind and body.

When confronted with a life-threatening crisis animals have a rapid input of adrenaline and an increased blood flow that prepares the body to fight, defend or run away. That is what survival is all about. In crisis situations much the same happens to people, and even when the crisis lessens or goes away, there is a release of those tensions with another set of emotions taking over. Be comfortable in knowing that it is normal to express emotion. When you have been hurt or upset it is acceptable to show that through your body language and to express those feelings provided that they are kept within reasonable bounds.

Human contact and interaction is charged with a variety of emotions. It is a normal way in which those relationships are expressed and developed. Emotions such as love, laughter, enjoyment and excitement can be very pleasurable. The manner in which someone reduces built-up tension and stress varies from person to person. For me, any combination of a good laugh, good company, good food, good music, a cuddle and a glass of good red have guaranteed success.

It is therefore important to transmit your feelings and emotions in such a manner that others can understand how you are reacting to the situation and the extent of the damage or benefit you have from it. It is also important to read your own feelings and to try to understand them. Try to avoid returning to the same situations that created the conflict in the first place. For each crisis try to work together to achieve a positive and cooperative outcome. Develop the future rather than dwell on the past. So many dispute resolution procedures are cut dead by constant reference to related and unrelated past incidents and associations. This achieves very little in your attempts to walk together to agreement and a positive outcome.

EMPATHY

Empathy is a relationship between people in which there is a flow and understanding of feelings and motives. Empathy produces a sensitivity and compassion towards, and understanding of, the other person that in turn allows for more effective communication. Having empathy for someone else does not mean that we must subjugate ourselves to their thinking or actions. It means that you can have respect for them even when they have different values, backgrounds, styles of operation and opinions. We will be able to work with these people even when they come from a different direction and we can value what they contribute to the process although it might differ from our own contributions.

In the best circumstances we can work with others on a level playing field in an open and honest atmosphere with each making positive contributions and with neither trying to dominate the other. It is easier to assess the various options without trying to denigrate them or be obsessed with protecting our own territory. The more you understand and respect the other person the more both of you will gain from the experience.

Empathy is the ether through which communication will pass. The more the empathy, sensitivity and compassion, the better the communication. Positive expressions of emotion will increase the empathy and breakdown, or remove blockages in the path of communication.

■ WHAT CAN WE CHANGE?

If we are to be more successful in handling conflict and difficult situations something must change. How easy it that? There are four basic alternatives:

1. *Change the world.*
2. *Change the organisation in which you work.*
3. *Change the other people with whom you work or associate.*
4. *Change yourself.*

1. *Since the time of Adam and Eve people have been trying to change the world to make it a better place in which to live. Yet, even after thousands of years, we have not even made a dent in the achievement of harmonious relationships on a world scale or relative equity for all people. All the political leaders will try to convince*

you that they have the answers, but you still tend to vote for those whom you believe will give you the best comparative advantage over other people or the least comparative disadvantage. In other words, in the real world, most of us are on about maintaining the difference. We can therefore put the first alternative in the too hard basket — impossible to achieve in our lifetime. It does not mean that we should give up trying, but as individuals we are not going to have a great impact.

2. *In the light of all of your experience, how easy have you found it to significantly change the organisation in which you work or the community in which you live? If it is similar to my lengthy experience then your answer is: very difficult to almost impossible. The system must be served. Organisations will change mostly as a result of a major external influence such as a change of government, a new competitor, a change to the supply of resources or markets, or a change of ownership — not from your actions from within. Our ability to make a significant change is virtually nil; again in the too hard basket. As the young people say: 'Get real.'*

3. *Look to the people with whom you have worked and at your partner, your friends and associates, and assess how easily it has been to significantly change their behaviour, style of operation and thinking. If you live or work with someone over a lengthy period there will be some convergence of thinking and practice over time, but it would be very rare to achieve a rapid change in another person's behaviour, thinking and practice. Your answer, therefore, will be in most cases: very difficult.*

4. *The only other alternative is to change the manner in which you approach conflict and its management.*
   - *We will change ourselves and the manner in which we approach other people.*
   - *We will try to understand our own behaviour first and how we impact on others.*
   - *We will attempt to take greater control of ourselves before we try to influence or control others.*
   - *We will not try to change others until we fully understand and change ourselves.*

When we have difficulties with others, or are in genuine conflict situations, we too often look for faults in them which, in turn, will justify our perception of their guilt and blame and our desire to change their behaviour. I want you now to look to your involvement in the conflict situation, assess your own behaviour and your approaches towards resolution. Do that before you attempt to change others.

WHAT ARE YOUR OPTIONS?
In a period of crisis or conflict you need to consider your options:
- If we don't like what is happening, is it possible to change it?

- If it is not possible to change it, are we willing to accept it?
- If we are not willing to accept it, are we willing to leave and walk away from it?
- If we do not have the option of walking away, is there another way to deal with it?

This might appear to you as too cold and ruthless an analysis of the options and so I invite you to seek another alternative. There will be hundreds of reasons why you cannot or will not walk away from a conflict or the situation in which you live or work and I am not suggesting that you should. In most situations, therefore, our focus will be on managing the situation, not walking away. In the worst situations, walking away might be the best option; but in the majority of disputes, walking away merely puts off the inevitable. It does not address the problem; it merely displaces it to reappear at a later time, here or in another place.

APPROACH FROM A DIFFERENT DIRECTION

The best managers see their only option is to change *their* approach to the handling of the problem or conflict and the manner in which they communicate with other people. The two traditional approaches to conflict are either aggressive confrontation or avoidance, neither of which has been proven to be a long-term solution. We need now to approach conflict from a different direction.

Those of you who are familiar with martial arts will realise that the basic principles involve discipline, focus and self-control, with an emphasis on defence and control rather than the attack and destroy methods portrayed in popular movies. In applying these same principles to difficult situations I suggest that you look to the following:

- Focus on the situation at hand.
- Carefully analyse the **facts**.
- Clear the **phoge**: **p**hilosophy, **h**earsay, **o**pinions, **g**ut feeling and **e**motion.
- Analyse the other person and the direction from which they are coming.
- Walk with them instead of at them.
- Try to identify their needs, concerns and anxieties.
- Look at the situation from their perspective. Put yourself in their shoes.
- Deal with the emotion, stress and aggression and separate them from the facts.
- Keep hold of your own agenda and focus on the desired outcomes.
- Use their energy to deflect and turn any attack.
- Having gained control of the situation, walk beside them and steer them towards a solution.

In this way you are more likely to work together towards a resolution instead of beating each other's brains to a pulp.

Now that you have a better understanding of the nature of conflict, the next chapter will walk you through a range of practical strategies from which you can choose the most appropriate to meet the situation at hand at any given time. A better understanding of the advantages and disadvantages of the various strategies will give you the confidence and courage to act quickly and effectively in any conflict situation.

chapter 3

Resolving conflict at work

- Assessment and analysis
- The joint problem-solving approach
- Drawing or mapping the conflict
- Strategies to manage conflict

■ ASSESSMENT AND ANALYSIS

A brief assessment of a conflict situation will help you arrive at the best way to resolve it. There are useful strategies and principles to apply at this stage.

DEALING WITH DIFFICULT PEOPLE

Too often in conflict situations one of the parties will attempt to adopt a coercive, directive attitude in which they will try to belittle and frighten the other person. Other people use different approaches to assume ascendancy over the other person. When you become involved in a conflict situation, whether as a party to the dispute or as a third party assisting in its resolution, you will have to deal with the expressions of power by the other people. In the emotional atmosphere of conflicts these people do not give up their power easily. What will you do when such a person confronts you and says 'No' to your proposal or gives you clear indications on where to go and how to get there?

Listen and ask questions for clarification and test your understanding of their concerns. Keep talking with them rather than at them. Assure them that you are willing to listen to their concerns and that you will attempt to resolve the issues raised. Try to establish a point of trust and confidence with them. Give them time and space to consider the options because any demand for instant agreement will be confronting and usually result in an instant refusal. When you have discussions with them, clarify your involvement, where you want the process to go and your expectations of them and others.

Look for opportunities to bring people together with other people in a joint problem-solving approach and indicate how they might contribute to the exercise. Recognise their fears and needs by putting yourself in their shoes. That does not mean that you will behave in the same manner, but it will give you a point of contact and understanding from which you can walk the person back to the table to continue the process of solving the problem. Take yourself to their side of the dispute and then walk back with them to a point of resolution.

Communicate with people at their level of understanding and at their level of involvement. Trying to negotiate at a level above their comprehension, training and experience, or in an area outside their immediate responsibility, will cause further confusion and ambiguity. This in turn will aggravate the conflict and make it more difficult to resolve.

Don't expect to win them all over to your desired outcomes, but at least try to get them to a situation where they can see that what you are putting to them is clear, fair, open, consistent, logical and is in accordance with the organisation's policies and guidelines, natural justice and legislation. If you bypass the guidelines and legislation in order to patch over a dispute for an easy solution, then others will expect you to do the same for them in the future and that will result in inconsistency and lack of respect for your guidelines. If your policies are at fault then change them, but don't manipulate them as a favour to some parties in the dispute.

Each person in a dispute tries to take up a position where they will have the greatest advantage or the least comparative disadvantage and will use one form or other of power, authority or influence to establish or maintain that position. In doing so they will try to influence you to gain an advantage for themselves. When you are aware of these pressures you will be able to refocus their attention and energies back to the real issues and the means by which they will be addressed. Highlight first any areas of common agreement. When they see that they are not in total disagreement, people will more easily move to the next point of agreement and resolution. Keep hold of the agenda.

So, in summary:

- When there is a real or perceived dispute gather the facts, clear the phoge (philosophy, hearsay, opinion, gut feeling, emotion) and focus on the real issues or problems.
- Research the situation, its background and underlying causes and don't be distracted by the symptoms on the surface.
- Set the compulsory and desirable outcomes of the resolution.
- Consider all of the possible strategies for resolution, taking into consideration the time, place, the people involved and the circumstances that led to the conflict.
- Evaluate the advantages and disadvantages of each strategy, the risks involved and the possible barriers to be overcome.
- Choose the strategy that is most likely to get the disputing parties to work together towards a common agreement and a commitment to put in place any necessary follow-up action.
- Monitor the implementation of any follow-up procedures agreed to by the parties.

ACTION RESEARCH AND ANALYSIS

The first basic principle applying to dispute resolution is the establishment of the facts. This is a formula that I particularly like:

Get the FACTS, clear the PHOGE.

Disputes are charged with emotion: some people play games to distract you towards their side of reason; others are so confused that they do not know how to act rationally. The stress and tension adds to that confusion and disorder. Political pressure and the overt displays of power, status and position are used to intimidate you towards a certain approach. Accusations, denials, counter-accusations and wild assumptions cast in an atmosphere of blame, guilt, threat, fear and aggression present to you a scene of utter chaos and confusion.

In these circumstances PHOGE (philosophy, hearsay, opinion, gut feeling, emotion) clouds reality. This acrostic represents the five factors that must be cleared away in order to get to the facts.

P: PHILOSOPHY? It is easy in the emotional atmosphere of a conflict situation to make sweeping general statements that assume the grandeur of truth and knowledge and hope that they act as a means of diverting other people's attention from the real issues.

'Well, we all know what women (men) are like. They really can't be trusted in difficult situations. They are so wrapped up in their own little worlds that they don't have time for anyone else. They can't see past the end of their nose. They only have one thing on their mind. They are all the same and you can't depend on them. You can't believe what they say, so don't take any notice of them.'

Comments like this make no positive contribution to the process and you should clear them away as quickly as possible and redirect people's focus back to the important issues and the means by which we can come to some agreement.

H: HEARSAY? 'Well, we all know what Harry is like. Someone was telling me only yesterday some stories about Harry that would make your hair curl. I have even heard a few things about him from people who worked with him at the other place. I have been told in confidence from a reliable source, and I want you to swear that you won't repeat it, that Harry was involved in something suspicious last year. I'm not at liberty to give you the details but I can assure you that it is the truth.'

There is not one single fact in that conversation and all of it should be thrown in the bin where it belongs. If the person wishes to pursue that line, ask them to provide concrete evidence of their allegations and the names of those who can corroborate their statements. Inform them that their allegations will be put to Harry so that he might have the opportunity to respond to them in the spirit of natural justice. When confronted, those gossip-mongers who thrive on promoting their own self-image through this approach will quickly fade away into the shadows.

O: WILD OPINIONS? If I had a dollar for every scatterbrained opinion expressed during intense negotiations or dispute procedures I would be a very rich man. However, others don't necessarily see their opinions as scatterbrained and might be putting them forward in good faith. It is up to you to test the quality of the opinion against the facts, evidence, policies, guidelines, best practice and the desired outcomes. When it does not meet these criteria clear it away and get back to basics.

G: GUT FEELING? '*I always had my suspicions about Mary. I have a nose for these things. I get a feeling in my bones. You have to follow your gut feeling because there is little else you can depend on these days. All this modern management theory is garbage. When you have been around as long as I have you depend on your instincts. It works every time. I must be right because the bosses keep changing but I'm still here.*'

If you are to have intuitive thoughts about an issue then do your research and test their veracity against the facts and the evidence. Otherwise your gut feelings are mere distractions and will make no valuable contribution to the resolution process.

E: EMOTIONS? As mentioned earlier, conflicts are charged with emotions that divert attention from what has to be done to achieve an agreed resolution. Manage the emotions first and then refocus on the issues at hand.

Stick to the **facts**. There is a danger in assuming that what is being told to you by a complainant is the truth and that you are expected to gather the evidence to confirm it, in order that appropriate action might follow against the other person in the conflict. Don't assume anything! Take any allegation, complaint or situation and investigate it by gathering facts and analysing the evidence. Try to establish if there is any corroboration to support or refute the allegations.

Give the person against whom the allegations have been made the opportunity to respond to them and for them to raise any other issues to be taken into consideration. It is natural justice for each person to be given the opportunity to defend themselves against allegations or charges and they must be given reasonable time to prepare their defence. They are innocent until proven guilty. It is unfair to assume guilt.

Too often someone will approach you with complaints about another person but will preface their approach with the statement:

'Look, I believe you should be made aware of the things Harry is doing and I want you to do something about it. Please don't tell Harry that I've told you and I don't want to be involved in any way because I just find it so stressful and I wouldn't like Harry to know that it was me who told you. I just want you to get rid of the problem so that we can get on with our jobs.'

Let these people know that you fully appreciate their concerns but make it clear that the allegations will be put to Harry for his response and that the matter will be investigated. Ask them to name other people who can corroborate their story. Clarify for them the options for resolving those issues and the role that they, Harry and you will take in the process.

■ THE JOINT PROBLEM-SOLVING APPROACH

If we are serious about managing conflict in the workplace we will shift our approach away from coercive, directive and arbitrary strategies and move towards a cooperative joint problem-solving approach. This approach can be adapted into any of the strategies outlined below, and the more we move this way the more permanent and positive will be the outcomes.

For this to be effective we need to become more involved in assisting the conflicting parties to identify the issues or problems. Thus we will gain their commitment to work together towards a joint solution and we will help them see that walking together towards a solution is better than the traditional headbutting, adversarial and points-scoring style of conflict resolution of the past.

In this collaborative model we will assist conflicting parties to identify their skills and experiences and to pool their collective wisdom and talent. We will encourage them to put all of the information on the table and to recommend strategies and options for resolution. We will attempt to redirect their negative destructive energy into more positive channels: towards a clear analysis of the situation, an evaluation of the various options and an assessment of the appropriate direction for solution.

Advise each person as to where they can seek further support, guidance and information.

At any stage the group might call in experts or seek more information to assist the process.

Seeking support, guidance and information does, however, mean that parties in the dispute have to come to terms with gaining a commitment to cooperation and collaboration. This is where you will play a major role in getting the momentum started. It is an advantage if the people involved are prepared or encouraged to use their high order thinking; to think laterally; to show initiative; and to be innovative. Think of a number of conflict situations and how their resolution might have taken a more positive approach had both parties been willing to work together towards a solution.

When there is a general problem concerning the staff bring them together in a joint problem-solving approach to the problem. You as the manager will use your skills as a leader to encourage participation, facilitate the process, coordinate the responses, provide information and resources and guide them to an agreed conclusion. In this way your research will be action based and will involve those people who have to put the solution into place.

During your training and development programs with staff, design case studies based on real problems of the workplace and ask the staff to use their combined knowledge, skills and experience to prepare appropriate strategies to deal with them. Add your greater experience to the pool of learning so that staff will have clearer expectations of what will happen in the event that a similar situation occurs in their unit. Their greater confidence in knowing what to do will focus their energies and efforts on positive outcomes rather than destructive negativity caused by confusion.

◼ DRAWING OR MAPPING THE CONFLICT

When police are investigating a major crime they will often commence by brainstorming all of the relevant matters and placing them on a board showing the relationships between them. Watch them do this in the good police shows on television. They prepare an overall schematic view of the scene and the various factors that might be relevant to the investigation. In fact, they are drawing a picture or a visual map of the scene and the circumstances surrounding the case.

In the same way, a conflict situation can be drawn or mapped so that it more clearly reveals the main issues in the dispute. It will more clearly identify the players, the facts, who said what to whom, who did what to whom, the interpersonal relationships, how the conflict developed and at what stage it is now. This will help to clear the way for resolution.

This process will help us to piece together the relevant matters in logical patterns. It will help us to show the important linkages. It will not only show us what we do know but, more importantly, what we do not know and when we have to do more research and information gathering to fill in the gaps. It will assist in identifying extraneous and irrelevant material that is clouding the issue and needs to be put aside. It helps us to move through the emotions and stress to the underlying causes of the dispute.

For most of us a picture, drawing or map is easier to read than a disconnected assortment of written notes or verbal messages. Our thinking and analytical processes are enhanced if we can see a visual, physical pattern. Its structures and relationships appear to be more tangible and logical and therefore easier to interpret.

When drawing or mapping a conflict, follow the 10-point plan outlined below.

STEP 1: INVESTIGATE AND GATHER THE INFORMATION
Look and see, listen and hear, question and analyse, think and understand. Interview all the relevant people in the dispute. Question, question, question and then attempt to test the veracity of your evidence against other information. Try to establish the **facts** and clear the **phoge**. Your credibility as someone who can handle conflict resolution will be established by the manner in which you carry out this important step. If others can see that you are open, honest, fair, transparent and unbiased at this stage they are more likely to walk with you through the remainder of the process. If you rush this step, make too many assumptions or show bias you will be exposed later. The time and space spent here will save time, space and further conflict later.

STEP 2: IDENTIFY THE REAL ISSUES, HIDDEN AGENDAS AND UNDERLYING CAUSES
Leaving a dirty coffee cup on the table might have been a trigger that ignited the conflict, but it was not the underlying cause of the conflict. It is merely the inflammation on the surface that indicated that there were other factors to be investigated. In the same way, personality clashes are indicators of a problem, not the problem itself. During a dispute

other issues will emerge that might not be directly related to the specific conflict at hand. Don't cloud the process at this stage with these issues. Put them aside to be dealt with at a later time.

Look particularly to relationships between the players and the manner in which people use power to influence or intimidate others. Question whether the display of conflict is displaced from somewhere else. If someone has had a fight with their partner this morning they might carry that anger to the workplace where they might vent it on someone else. Is there a medical reason why someone might find it difficult to get along with others? Summarise the issues as presented by each of the participants. Feed back your interpretation of the issues to test their understanding of them and to ensure that you are focused on the real substance of the conflict. Explain to them why the other extraneous matters will not remain on the agenda.

STEP 3: PUT IT IN THE APPROPRIATE CONTEXT
Try to identify the area, section, unit or environment in which the conflict occurred and developed. In some cases, a minor dispute might be made out to be much larger than it is because one or both people want to give the impression that they are not the only ones involved. In other cases, what appears to be a minor dispute between two people might be a reflection of a deeper problem of poor management, lack of guidance and training.

STEP 4: IDENTIFY THE PARTICIPANTS
Clearly identify those in the first row of the conflict and then show the relationship of the others to the main participants. Eliminate those on the fringe who cannot contribute to the resolution, especially those Mexican wavers who are there only to enjoy the spectacle and the prospect of a bloodbath. Clarify each participant's perception of the problem. Consider their needs, concerns, relationships and what they can contribute to the truth of the matter.

STEP 5: ANALYSIS
Having gathered the facts, analyse them and put them in logical patterns. Show the relationships and then determine whether it is necessary to seek further information and, if so, where it can be found. Use the information to test the validity of the issues raised by the participants. Look for inconsistencies and gaps. Show how one piece of information can corroborate others. Isolate information that cannot be corroborated and those situations when there is a disagreement based on one person's word against another's. Take each issue in turn rather than trying to deal with the whole dispute in one go. It is easier to climb a number of small hills than to tackle Mount Everest in one go.

STEP 6: CLEARLY IDENTIFY ANY COMMON GROUND

Identify points of agreement between the parties. Confirm with all parties those facts, issues and other matters for which there is agreement. In particular, identify options for solutions that are agreed to by all or most of the parties. This can be a good starting point towards resolving the problem because at least these matters have their agreement. The sooner you can establish that there is some agreement the sooner you can get the disputants to walk together towards resolution.

STEP 7: ESTABLISH A WILLINGNESS AND COMMITMENT TO MOVE TOWARDS RESOLUTION AND AGREEMENT

Try to obtain the agreement of the parties that there is a problem, then an agreement to the nature of the problem and then a commitment, that they recognise to be in their own best interests, to work together towards an agreement. Are there any indicators that this is possible? While there are some disagreements on interpretation, look for any commitment or willingness to resolve the situation. Try to establish in their minds that you will assist them to work together in solving the problem and that it will be for the benefit of all concerned. As a last resort, in more serious cases, you might have to spell out the sanctions or penalties of not working together towards agreement.

STEP 8: CANVASS THE RANGE OF POSSIBLE STRATEGIES FOR RESOLUTION

Try to involve all parties in designing strategies for resolution. Each party will be more committed if they feel that they have had input into the outcomes and agreement. The best resolutions are those for which there is agreement and commitment between the parties. These are usually more effective than those that result in an order given by a third party when neither party is committed to the order. Don't be restricted to only one course of action. The resolution might involve a combination of strategies. Look to the options outlined later in this chapter.

STEP 9: AGREEMENT

When both parties have reached agreement, lock it down and, if necessary, have each party sign that agreement. Build in a time line with appropriate ongoing monitoring. Identify the support structures that will be there to assist the parties to implement the follow though.

STEP 10: MONITOR THE FOLLOW-UP

Build into your plan the means by which the implementation of the strategies can be monitored and modified as the need arises.

FIGURE 3.1
Drawing and mapping the conflict

Issues	Information
FACTS	PHOGE
Context/environment	
Main players	Their needs, concerns, anxieties
Other players	Their relationship to each other
Analysis	
Common agreement	
Unresolved matters, hidden agendas	More information needed
Strategies for resolution	
Actions to be taken following agreement	Who is to be involved?
What is the recommended time line?	Monitoring

■ STRATEGIES TO MANAGE CONFLICT

There is no single magic solution to dealing with all conflicts. There are many different approaches you might take to handle a problem and you will select the one that will be most appropriate at the time, according to the circumstances and the people involved. You might even change the strategy during the process. It is important to understand the advantages and disadvantages of a range of options and the circumstances in which each will have the desired effect so that you will be able to choose the one best suited to the occasion.

Before you make a decision as to the most appropriate approach, assess the alternatives and then select the one most suited to that dispute, in that context, at that time involving those people. Look now at the following dispute handling strategies and apply them in hindsight to ones in which you have been involved or have observed. Assess whether each particular strategy would have been appropriate to the particular dispute and how it would have affected the outcomes for all parties involved. Compare each with the approach that was taken in each case.

Don't be fazed by terms such as arbitration, conciliation and mediation, which might appear to be more appropriate to a much higher and more formal level of dispute resolution than your humble level of supervision. While these processes are carried on in courts and tribunals at the highest levels, they are also appropriate in certain circumstances in the workplace in everyday operations. Gain an understanding of each process so that you have a range of options and can choose the most appropriate one for each situation.

Whatever strategies you adopt, the common objective is to move the various participants towards resolution by common agreement. This can best be achieved if you obtain a commitment from them that there is a problem, that they agree on the nature of the problem and that it is best that they work together with your guidance towards a resolution. They must also be committed to the follow-up. This might sound easier said than done and, in some cases, it is extremely difficult, but the alternative of doing nothing is not an option. Selecting the most appropriate strategies from the following options will give you the confidence and courage to act, and achieving success will accelerate that lift in confidence for further actions.

COUNSELLING

Counselling is very effective in the early stages of a dispute or as a preliminary to a more major process. It is a process that will be part of your everyday people management and when others see it in this light, it is a natural part of the environment and does not generate the anxieties and fear that a one-off consultation creates. It will be a normal part of your guidance, mentoring and development of those who report to you or with whom you work. It is also a vital element in all of the other strategies outlined below.

There will be many occasions when you could be approached for advice and support in difficult situations. You will often be asked for guidance from people who work in your area or from colleagues in other areas. In taking on that role you will be in a position to assist them to clarify the issues and the possible outcomes. Help them to come to terms with handling their own problem. Act in the same manner as a mediator or conciliator rather than as an arbitrator. You might suggest to them a number of options and, together with them, brainstorm the advantages and disadvantages of each option.

Avoid becoming entwined in their emotions. You should not be seen as being totally supportive of their anger and resentment against another party. Be objective in walking them through the stress towards more positive outcomes and resolutions. Help them to look at themselves and the other people in the dispute. Clarify in the first instance that it is not your role to make judgments or take sides and that others must be given the opportunity to respond to the allegations and have the opportunity to present their own case and suggestions for change.

Be careful not to move into professional fields for which you have no expertise, training or experience. In some conflict situations there could be an underlying factor of physical, psychological or psychiatric disorder with one of the parties. While you might involve yourself in gathering the facts that point to this condition you should avoid further involvement in prescribing the remedies. Bring in the experts. Do not try to be an amateur psychologist. Try to distinguish that point where the psychology of good management gives way to the need for professional expertise in this area. If in doubt seek further advice before proceeding.

Counselling, if well conducted, will break down the normal barriers between staff, supervisors and managers because people will see it as a support mechanism that works.

Conflicts often develop because people, mainly through inexperience or lack of knowledge, cannot or will not see alternatives to their current stance. It is your knowledge, skills, experience and managerial expertise that will provide the necessary guidance and support to walk these people through the issue towards a positive resolution. When your efforts have been successful, their respect for you will lift through the roof.

MEDIATION

Mediation is an alternative means of dispute resolution that is becoming more frequently used in a range of situations. It involves a third party assisting the process but, in this strategy, the person does not make decisions or recommendations as in arbitration or conciliation. The mediator controls or facilitates the process. They will assist by clarifying the issues to be addressed, determining who will speak and when they will speak, organising the place and setting of the meeting and the conduct of that meeting.

Mediation is a means by which you, as the independent facilitator, can assist the others to focus on a joint problem-solving approach to their differences. There will be numerous occasions when you will be effective as an independent mediator assisting others to solve problems. On other occasions you might be a party to a dispute and, when your differences cannot be resolved by negotiation, you might suggest to the other person that, together, you invite a third party to assist the process.

As far as possible the mediator should try to be independent even though at times it may be difficult to appear to be so — especially when the disputants are both from your area or work unit. In its purest sense, mediation does not allow the third party to recommend or decide the outcomes or the direction that the agreement should take. This has the positive aspect of encouraging each side to contribute to the final agreement and therefore have greater commitment to its follow-up actions. At times this aspect is the most frustrating for the mediator especially when one or both parties are intransigent. At times the path to resolution seems very obvious to you as a mediator but it not obvious to the others who are so emotionally involved that they cannot think logically and clearly. They might not have access to vital information or they might not have the skills necessary to negotiate on equal terms with the other side.

I will confess to you that when I an involved in mediation, I tend to use some of the advantages and processes of conciliation to get the process moving. It's better than banging their heads together to clarify their vision. I use questions to focus their attention on developing an agreed resolution.

'John, I want you to think about the proposal that Mary has just put forward. Do you see any value in that proposal? Is there any part that you would like to change? How would you change it? Is there anything you would add to improve it? Mary. John has now proposed a variation to your suggestion that appears to have some merit. Would you be willing to alter your proposal along those lines?'

Whenever one party or the other presents an option that appears to have value, focus their attention on building or modifying that proposal. In that way they can at least concentrate on something concrete and shift their energies and emotions from negative attack to cooperative production. Provided that you offer the alternatives as options for consideration and not as orders or directions it will be still in the spirit of mediation.

Mediation can be conducted informally or formally, depending on the seriousness of the dispute and the willingness of the parties to participate. It is probably best to use the informal approach early in a dispute as it is less threatening and is more likely to result in a speedy resolution with least disruption to each side. The formal approach is used in more serious cases or when the conflict has developed to extremes of behaviour, high emotion and antagonism or when numerous other attempts to get the parties together have failed.

As an independent mediator I have found it helpful to meet with each person separately. I listen to their complaints and try to crystallise these into issues of concern. It is important to feed back your interpretation to ensure its accuracy. This is a listening, questioning and feedback exercise.

Arrange a suitable meeting place that is comfortable and non-threatening. Clarify to both parties how the meeting will be conducted and how and when they will take an active part. Encourage them to avoid 'you' statements and to concentrate on how they see the issues and their desired outcomes. Emphasise that each will have an equal opportunity to participate and a chance to respond to the issues and proposals of the other person. Throughout the meeting encourage both parties to concentrate on 'I' statements with the emphasis on what each person is willing to contribute. Discourage 'you' statements that are accusatory and demanding of the other person.

Try to commence the first meeting with agreements.

'Do you agree that this matter has been going on for too long? Has it had a negative effect on both of you? Is it affecting your work? Is it affecting other people? Do you agree that, if it continues, it will be more damaging? Do you want to resolve this matter? Do you agree that mediation is the way to come to a satisfactory resolution? Do you both agree to me being the mediator to assist you through this process?'

Already they have agreed seven times. That is a positive start especially when they probably have not agreed on anything for some time.

Break up the proceedings into a number of bite-sized sections. Do not try to deal with the whole dispute at one time because it will be as daunting as climbing Mount Everest. Take each small issue separately, as this will be more like climbing a hill than a mountain. In their minds a resolution will now appear achievable. In the early stages it helps to get them working together on brainstorming ideas and proposals, with you assisting in controlling their emotions, eliminating irrelevant matters and encouraging a cooperative effort.

Time and space are very valuable factors in a resolution or problem-solving process. So often the intensity of emotions is so great that the people can't see the trees for the forest and it is advisable to occasionally call a break to have them focus on a particular issue or proposal in private. If you insist that they remain in the room where there is a lot of emotion, aggravation and duress they are more likely to come out fighting like cornered animals. Time and space will provide a cooling-off period.

When they return they will be more likely to focus on the possible resolution rather than attacking the other person. People need time to consider the options put to them. They need space to test the proposals and to gather further information. They will need to structure modifications or alternatives to those proposals and to discuss them in private before coming back to the meeting.

Keep asking questions and feed back their answers to allow both parties to hear what they are saying or proposing. Cut short any matters that cannot be resolved. Put them aside so that they don't cloud the main agenda. For example, they might disagree on what each said during a telephone conversation. If there is no corroborating evidence there is no way that the matter can be resolved and nothing will be gained by continuing the rage. Get them to agree to disagree and put it aside. Use your 180-degree vision to anticipate the likely reactions of each person in order that you can move to address it in advance. Ask each person to think what it would be like to be in the other person's position. Ask them to consider the effect that the proposals will have on them. Diffuse the desire of each to punish the other side.

It assists resolution if you halt the proceedings from time to time to summarise progress and to refocus on the next issue. Sometimes it is advisable to meet again later, provided that you give them a specific issue or proposal to consider for the next meeting. Conclude the proceedings by giving a copy of the agreement to both people with an agreed time line for implementation of any follow-up action. Name those who might be involved in providing support, counselling and development in the future.

Advantages of mediation
- The mediator is independent.
- The parties work together towards resolution.
- There is a greater commitment to achieving the outcomes.
- It is a joint problem-solving approach.
- It is a controlled process.
- It is less expensive and traumatic than legal proceedings.

Disadvantages of mediation
- It can be time-consuming.
- It can be more difficult when there is an imbalance of power between the parties.
- It takes time for people to accept it as a positive strategy.

NEGOTIATION

Negotiation is the process by which two people or parties talk with each other, raise issues, explore options and hopefully reach a common agreement. No third party is involved. You are negotiating every day of your life. Think of all the occasions at home, in the community or at work where you and another person discuss alternatives each and every day. Most of the time we do it without thinking. On most occasions our negotiations are low key and friendly and we come to an agreement with the minimum of fuss or stress.

If we ask a group of people if they like bargaining most will say that it is embarrassing and that they prefer not to be involved. Yet, in the real world, those same people are constantly bargaining or negotiating several times a day. They will do it in shops, with their partner, at sport, with their neighbours and at work. It could be as simple as who will drive the car or as complex as a major property and custody settlement following divorce or enterprise bargaining at work.

The successful management of almost every dispute, grievance and conflict and the resolution of problems will involve an element of negotiation even when a third party is involved.

So the knowledge and skills of the process and practice of negotiation are essential elements of your leadership qualities. All your technical and professional expertise will have little value in the reality of the workplace if you cannot negotiate with those around you. On a day-to-day basis you negotiate with those to whom you report, your colleagues, staff, clients, customers, suppliers, government authorities, community associations and members of the public. Each of these contacts has the potential for disagreement and conflict and will therefore highlight the importance of your ability to negotiate.

Negotiation is a process of communication involving interaction and reaction. It starts from a point of difference or polarisation of ideas, values or practice that has resulted in disagreement. In extreme cases the parties are either charging one another like mountain goats or are turning away from each other and rapidly moving further apart. In these extremes it is difficult for both of them to agree to sit down to discuss their concerns or to negotiate their differences.

> 'Go away. I don't even want to talk to you.'
> 'I'm so disgusted I won't have anything to do with you.'
> 'I am not going to put up with your threats any longer.'
> 'You are always trying to get on my right side so that you get your own way. Get lost.'

The object of negotiation is for both parties to recognise their differences, then to agree to resolve them in a situation where both are able to put their case, after which they will work together towards an agreed position. To be effective there has to be a commitment by both parties to want to solve their problems and differences even though each will be striving to gain the most and give up the least. Successful negotiations require each group to consider the other's proposals, to accept, reject or modify them and then propose the alternatives for the other to consider. Eventually, if successful, they will move towards a common position and agreement.

The two key words in negotiations are **if** and **then**. **If** I accede to your unreasonable demands, **then** I will expect you to agree to my unacceptable offer.

> *'If I agree to you having the computer at your work station then I would expect you to let me have the mobile phone with WAP and a Palmtop.'*
>
> *'I think that is unfair because I have to be out of the office often and need them myself. However, if I were to agree to that proposal then I would demand a new modern work station.'*
>
> *'I can't afford that because I have to purchase a new car; but if I were to agree then I would want you to accept that the new work station be in lieu of your annual bonus.'*
>
> *'No way. I worked hard for my bonus;, but, if I were to consider it I would ask for the use of the office car on the nights when I do overtime.'*

Try a simple exercise. You and a friend should work together on this one. Put a valuable item such as a watch or a piece of jewellery on the table. You are not allowed to speak and the only thing you can write down is the amount you are willing to offer and the counter-offer by the other person. You may use body language but no words are to be spoken. How long does it take you to agree on a price?

In the beginning the owner will demand a very high price for the item. This is their ambit claim and sets the upper limit. In return you will offer a ridiculously low price, which sets the lower limit. You will then proceed to negotiate an agreement between those limits. There is a zone in the middle that is determined, on the one hand, by the price above which you will not negotiate and, on the other hand, by a second, lower price below which the other person will not drop. This middle zone is where the serious negotiation takes place and the only place where agreement can be reached. If the lowest sum the seller is prepared to accept is greater than the highest sum you are prepared to pay then agreement cannot be reached and vice versa. It is easy to visualise this when we are negotiating the sale of a tangible, visible item such as a watch. It is more difficult when we are discussing matters such as working conditions, although the same basic principles apply to both.

FIGURE 3.2
Reaching towards agreement

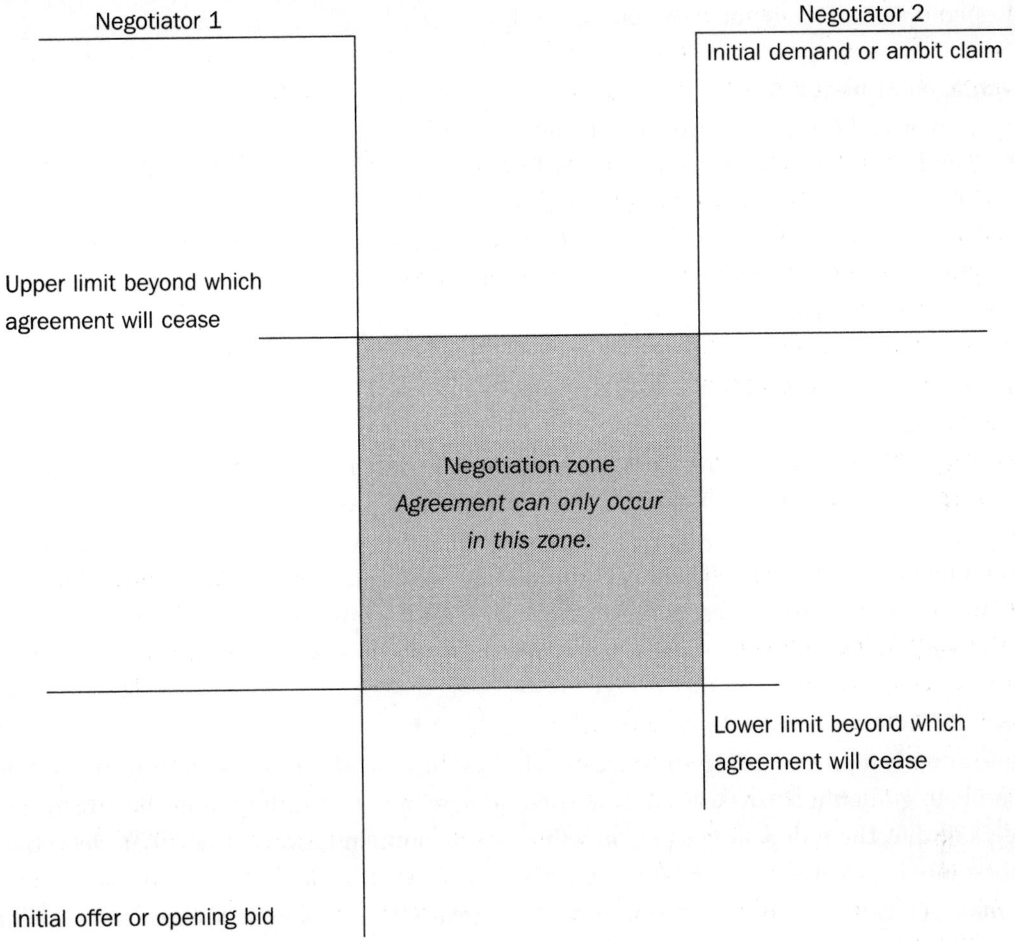

Negotiator 1

Negotiator 2

Initial demand or ambit claim

Upper limit beyond which
agreement will cease

Negotiation zone
*Agreement can only occur
in this zone.*

Lower limit beyond which
agreement will cease

Initial offer or opening bid

Negotiation is a process by which the parties reach agreement by resolving their differences. It does require some degree of trust because no other parties are involved. The best negotiations take place when there is respect on each side for the other person, an appreciation of where they are coming from, and an understanding of the pressures they are facing. When you are bargaining in some shops in Asia you will lose face and respect if you lose your temper and control. The same basic principle applies when you are bargaining in the workplace. If you cannot come to agreement through one-to-one negotiation, then look for another strategy to solve the problem. When you have conducted the negotiation in the spirit of good faith, openness and honesty, the respect that is generated will keep the process alive and will allow for flexibility as the need arises. When there is a high level of trust, negotiators can talk off the record and that in turn will open up hidden agendas and facilitate settlement.

Advantages of negotiation
- It involves both parties directly in the process.
- It is their decision, not that of a third party.
- There is a sense of ownership. Both parties know the resolution is theirs.
- There is a better understanding and appreciation of the other side.
- It will expose the reasons for deep-seated feelings.
- It will bring out hidden agendas.

Disadvantages of negotiation
- It can be very time-consuming.
- It requires a commitment from both parties to participate.
- If prolonged it can be costly, as in extended enterprise bargaining.
- Some people are disadvantaged by poor negotiation skills and lack of experience.
- Some people lack the confidence and courage to negotiate on equitable terms.
- There can be imbalances in power, authority and influence.
- There can be inequities in resources and access to information.

CONCILIATION
Conciliation is a process in which the disputing parties put their case to a third party who attempts to guide them towards a resolution and agreement. It differs from the arbitration process in that the independent person will make recommendations rather than decisions; although in a formal framework those recommendations are like a de facto decision. You, as a manager, can use the conciliation process to great effect in the workplace across a wide range of disputes from the simple to the more serious. It is usually far more informal than a court environment and the conciliator is bound less by laws, policies and procedures and more by common sense. A good conciliator will take the opportunity to break the formal proceedings to allow both parties time and space to consider various proposals, to conduct more research, gather information or consult others.

The conciliator acts more as a facilitator rather than a judge and, if they see value in a proposal, will suggest to the other party that they might give it serious consideration. In this way they can look beyond the dispute and its high emotion to the possible resolution and agreement. The best conciliators sense when to pause, break or accelerate according to the mood and momentum of the meeting.

As a conciliator be confident in asking questions of either side to clarify issues, discover what each side wants for themselves. Clarify their expectations of the others and seek their support for positive proposals. Be clear in your direction, particularly when a proposal is unacceptable. Use your personal power and influence and extensive knowledge and experience to guide and control the meetings in a manner that generates trust and confidence in your management. Their willingness to walk with you to agreement and resolution will depend on that trust.

This is a process that is used in a more formal sense in the Industrial Commission where every attempt is made to reach an agreement with the cooperation and participation of the disputants, rather than it being decided by arbitral decision in the formal court. In the workplace you can use a conciliation strategy in reasonably serious cases as long as both parties agree to work with you towards a resolution and have trust and confidence in your ability to keep control and treat both parties with equity and fairness. In serious cases you might attempt a conciliation process rather than pass it on to a formal disciplinary hearing. This emphasises the importance of solving the problems as close to the workplace and source of the dispute as possible.

Conciliation can be a very effective tool in the workplace, especially when you use the flexibility that the process allows. In many dispute situations in the past I have used a combination of conciliation and mediation to very good effect by tightening or loosening the control and direction of the discussions as the need arises and the mood and momentum allows. By using this approach you can fully utilise the benefits of the involvement and empowerment encouraged by mediation, but blend that with firmer control and guidance when frustration demands a more direct intervention.

Advantages of conciliation
- There is an independent third party.
- It is less threatening than arbitration.
- It is less bound by law and precedent.
- It is not so confrontationist.
- It attempts to get the parties to talk with each other.
- The parties feel they are contributing more to the outcomes.
- It places options on the table for consideration.
- It is more flexible.
- It uses the guidance and expertise of the conciliator.
- It sets strong direction through recommendation.
- It provides time and space for research and information gathering.

Disadvantages of conciliation
- Recommendations are from a third party.
- The parties not necessarily committed to the recommendations.
- It has a quasi-legal atmosphere.
- There is the disguised threat of penalty if they don't agree.

- It does not require an agreement.
- It is often seen as merely a pause or cooling off in the dispute.

MODIFIED ARBITRATION

It is far more sensible to have disputants try to work together towards an agreement under the guidance of a conciliator or mediator than to move immediately into the formal arbitration process with its heavy legal overtones.

There is a very strong movement in all walks of life today towards alternative dispute resolution procedures. You will notice this particularly in areas such as divorce and custody settlements, neighbourhood disputes, local government, land and environment proceedings, building services and consumer rights. It is also most appropriate for use in the workplace by you, the leader of the group, in dealing with difficult situations. It is far less traumatic a process and it can lead to greater understanding and cooperation between you and those with whom you associate.

Industrial commissions and courts will often recommend or direct the participants to conciliation or mediation and will only proceed with the formal court hearings should the other strategy not be successful. The conciliator or mediator concentrates on getting the negotiation between the parties moving by refocusing their attention to a joint approach to agreement, and, in addition, provides a setting in which each person has a fair hearing. The role of the conciliator is to assist the participants to reach an agreement that is acceptable to them and will satisfy the requirements of the court. Should no agreement be reached, the dispute will return to the court where it will be resolved through formal arbitration.

The best practitioners in the workplace use alternative dispute resolution procedures rather than the more formal courts or tribunals. They find the results far more effective and cost efficient in the long term. Re-emergence of the same types of disputes without dealing with the underlying causes and where the opposing sides do not commit themselves to the settlement will become like a cancer in your organisation. Dispute resolution strategies allow you to try the joint cooperative approach first knowing that, should it not be successful, you can refer the matter to a more formal arbitrary hearing.

Advantages of modified arbitration
- It is usually a more intimate and less threatening atmosphere than in court.
- It usually costs much less because it cuts back on the lengthy involvement of legal experts.
- It aims to reach a commitment to an agreed outcome instead of an imposed order from the court.
- The people work under the guidance of the mediator.
- They are informed of the costs and implications should they prefer to go to court and therefore understand the alternative.

- They mostly agree to mediation — a starting point to further agreement.
- The mediator will help to reduce or eliminate irrelevant issues.

Disadvantages of modified arbitration
- Some might use the process to gain an advantage before going to court.
- Some might feel that they have to give too much in order to achieve agreement.
- Many find negotiations and bargaining very stressful.
- Many feel they do not have the skills to negotiate.
- Some hope that a court decision will be fairer and give them a better chance.
- Some believe that the court will punish the other side for their perceived wrongs.
- If not managed well it can be a time-consuming exercise.
- Some will see the mediator as biased and part of the problem.
- Sometimes there is a tendency to shoot the messenger.

REPRESENTATIVE ARBITRATION
Representative arbitration is a strategy whereby each side to the dispute is represented on a panel that is convened by an independent third party. It is used more often in a formal sense for hearings relating to inefficiency, improper conduct, sexual harassment or other major concerns. It is a method often used in public sector employment. It can be an effective strategy in cases where someone appeals against a decision. It is a strategy that can be used effectively on an informal basis in the workplace.

In reality, each of the representatives tends to take the side of their group and the outcome will depend very much on the influence of the convener and their ability to bind the panel into a united decision, taking into consideration the facts, legislation, policies and procedures. When there is no agreement between the representatives on the panel the convener will have the casting vote on the decision.

If you are the convener, it will be important to control the process and to train the representatives in the manner in which the hearing will be conducted. Clarify their role in the decision-making process. Emphasise that they are the independent judges, not the disputants, and that they must recognise the rules of law and evidence and that both sides are to be treated fairly and equitably. They must restrain their desire to attack or intimidate the other side or be seen to act exclusively as an advocate for their side. The best panel members can rise above friendships and associations and make the right decisions for the right reasons. People of this quality are confident in explaining the panel's decision to their side knowing that it is right, even when it has gone against them.

This approach has much the same advantages and disadvantages as formal arbitration but has the added benefit that each party has a representative on the decision-making panel and, therefore, feels that they will get a fair hearing. This method of dispute resolution does highlight the advantages and good practice of allowing parties to the dispute to have access to support. People without this access can be intimidated by the other side, especially when that other person is in a more senior position and can bring to bear the weight of seniority and maybe the power and authority of hire and fire. A good convener will guide the process more to one of joint problem-solving rather than the more formal structure of a court hearing. In fact the best operators achieve the ideal of having everyone working together to identify the problems and then cooperate to find an agreed resolution. When this happens there is a greater commitment to the outcomes.

ARBITRATION

This is a process in which the conflicting parties can't agree and the process is taken over by a third party. That third person will listen to each side and then make a decision that is binding on both combatants. The classic example of arbitration is the court proceedings in which the judge or magistrate listens to the evidence presented by both sides and then makes a binding decision.

While arbitration in its purest form is conducted in a court or tribunal, the process can be used in a less formal setting, with decisions being made to settle disputes on the run. Consider the manner in which those in authority use arbitration as a means of settling disputes in the workplace on a day-to-day basis without proceeding to a formal hearing.

'You can't use Mary Jones in your section today because I have a backlog to clear by tomorrow morning and, besides, you had her for the last week.'

'I only used her last week to do that important job for the boss and that is still not finished. I have to have her today to meet the deadline tonight.'

'That's a laugh. You just want her to make up for the deadheads in your section, the ones you're afraid to do anything about.'

'You only want her so that you can impress the big chief so that it will look better for your application for that new job.'

At that stage, the director intervenes. 'I have listened long enough to your bickering. Daniel, you will have Mary until 11 o'clock this morning. Elizabeth, you will have her until this afternoon. Tomorrow I will have her working on a new project in my office. And remember, I want those priorities on my desk tomorrow morning and don't think that you are using overtime to complete the tasks. That's it, now get on with it.'

'But we have so much backlog to catch up.'

'That's not fair. The chief will not be happy if that project is not complete.'

'You have heard what I have said and my decision is final. You could have had the jobs half done if you had not stood around arguing about them.'

This is a simple case of arbitration in practice. It reflects the advantages and disadvantages of such a process.

Advantages of arbitration
- It is quick in coming to a decision.
- It is relatively inexpensive.
- The third party provides an independent input.
- When others can't agree someone else will decide.
- There will be a definite decision.
- There will be a clear course of action to follow.
- Everyone knows the outcomes should they not follow the decision.

Disadvantages of arbitration
- There has been no agreement to the problem.
- The decision has been handed down.
- Neither party has to be committed to the spirit of the decision.
- It has legalistic overtones.
- There are usually negative penalties or sanctions.
- It is adversarial and confrontationist.
- The problem is not necessarily solved.
- The enmity will emerge again in the same or a different context.

In the workplace the use of arbitration as an effective strategy is applied best in either the handling of minor day-to-day operational disputes or in major disciplinary hearings. On any day in the workplace there will be minor disagreements regarding such matters as processes, use of resources, working conditions, applications for special consideration or variations to routine. Provided the guidelines are relatively clear and there is some urgency in getting on with the job you, as the leader, will make quick decisions in regard to the dispute. You will be conscious, however, of the need to revisit it later on should the parties not be satisfied with the outcome. In the meantime the arbitral decision allows the work to continue while further research and analysis is completed on the subject.

Arbitration is also applied when there has been a serious breach of discipline or when a person appeals against a decision such as dismissal or non-selection for a position. Many managers consider that it is a waste of time to conduct formal hearings and that the staff member should be summarily dismissed. Increasingly they are finding that, should they fail to conduct internal hearings, they will have to answer to a higher court where they do not have control and their management comes under intense scrutiny. Major industrial disputes in the workplace, including disputes involving pay and working conditions, if unresolved, will be transferred to the Industrial Commission or court where a commissioner or judge will make an arbitral decision.

The best managers do everything in their power and influence to try to reach an agreement by using other strategies at the workplace. They prefer this to going to a court for settlement because they see, under those circumstances, that the dispute is not solved:

merely stalled to re-emerge at a later date in a different context.

The following chapter will guide you in assessing your workplace with a view to developing an environment in which conflict is least likely to occur and one where it is better managed when it does occur. It also presents a range of best practices as a guide for implementation.

chapter 4

Setting up programs

- Analyse the workplace
- Clarify policies and procedures
- Follow best practice

A conflict-free environment will not happen by itself. It is created, maintained, managed and developed by you. If we are to make it happen, we must plan for, implement and monitor a number of programs, policies and procedures in cooperation with our staff. In this chapter I have outlined for you a number of suggested approaches.

■ ANALYSE THE WORKPLACE

The first principle of success for the implementation of any program is to be committed to the purpose of that program and to show others that you are willing to back up that commitment with positive involvement and action. Be prepared to stand up in public and promote the program and its benefits; be open and honest with your audience; provide all the necessary information and be willing to answer questions, in public and privately. Stand up and tell everyone that you are committed to creating a cooperative productive workplace in which conflict is least likely to occur and that, when it does happen, it will be resolved as quickly as possible in a collaborative manner. Be willing to make adjustments to incorporate positive ideas raised by the staff. You are not the font of all knowledge and understanding and there is benefit in tapping into and utilising the pool of talent available to you from the team. Promote the changes with your boss and colleagues and try to get their commitment and support for your changes.

You will gain more commitment from the staff if you are willing to involve them in the design of programs and give them credit for their contributions. Allocate responsibilities to key members and involve them in assisting with the communication, training and the promotion of the various programs. Allocate sufficient resources to get the programs started and to provide for the training of all staff. Phase in the implementation of each program to allow time for its ongoing evaluation and modification. Be sufficiently flexible to allow for changes to meet the practical needs of the workplace. Promote the values of the program at staff meetings, training programs or with a special launch.

Encourage the chief general manager to publicly commit his or her approval and support for the programs because, without it, others will be less inclined to be involved. Keep everyone informed as to the success of programs and the modifications that are put in place to improve their effectiveness. Prepare reports and promote their success in newsletters or journals. When you have this level of commitment and the staff see that they are involved in positive programs that are being recognised publicly they will be more willing to be seen as part of them and bask in any reflected glory.

When this happens, others will come seeking support and guidance and the staff will see that this reflects further on their credibility. This will have a positive accelerator effect on the specific program and on the general area that you supervise.

ASSESS THE WORKPLACE

Get the staff together to conduct an environmental analysis with the prime objective of improving the workplace in order to reduce conflict to a minimum and to develop improved programs for the handling of disputes and conflicts. You might like to invite other people such as the managing director, the HR manager, a trusted colleague or an outside consultant to participate, provided they can contribute positively to the exercise. You will need to outline some limits such as budget and staff allocations to prevent the discussions flying off into dream world with statements such as: 'Well, we could do all of these wonderful things if they would only give us more money, equipment and staff.'

I suggest that you ban the word 'problem'. Emphasise that other groups have problems, we resolve them. I once banned the word 'problem' in the workplace and insisted that anyone who used it would have to contribute to a morning tea. It forced people to think in a different frame of mind. 'There is an issue that I would like to discuss...'; 'There is a procedure I believe we should revise...'; 'I would like to canvass some ideas regarding changes to...'; 'I feel we need to consider further development in...'. The staff were much amused to find that I was the worst offender for using the forbidden word and it cost me dearly at the local French patisserie.

WHERE WE ARE NOW

Take the staff through a **WHAT**? (**w**ell, **h**urdles, **a**ltered, **t**ake-off) exercise.

Step 1: What are we doing Well?

Individually and then in pairs, ask the staff to identify what they believe have been the main achievements of the group. Have the total group put these in some priority order. Keep promoting these achievements. Give the staff the confidence that you also confirm what they are doing well. Put the list on the wall for everyone to see.

Step 2: What are the Hurdles and hazards?

Ask the staff to identify the hurdles, hazards, log jams, fires and mud that have made it difficult to achieve our objective of a cooperative, collaborative and conflict reduced working environment. Avoid the word 'problem'. Focus their minds on the number of these hurdles that might be reduced or eliminated. Work with them to keep their focus on reducing the hazards.

Step 3: What has Altered?

Identify what has altered or changed in the organisation or what has happened in the outside world that has affected the workplace. Again focus the staff on the positive aspects of change and the possibilities or opportunities that will come from those changes. Even when there is some negative criticism about change, ask the staff to develop the best means to overcome those negative aspects.

Step 4: What has to be done to reach Take-off?

Ask each person to list the main areas of the workplace that need to be developed to improve working relationships in order to handle disputes and change direction to a more positive approach. Get people to pair up and combine their lists, reducing the list so it contains the five most important areas. Two pairs then will combine their lists, and then the total group will decide the most important five areas for development.

WHERE WE WANT TO BE

Break up the staff into five diverse groups and allocate one area to each group. Ask each group to work on their key area for development in four stages.

1. *Outline the nature and extent of the issue.*

2. *What is the background? Why has it become an area of concern?*

3. *What strategies will we use to improve this area?*

4. *What support will be required to improve this area and who will be involved at this level?*

After each stage the groups should walk around and observe what each of the other groups has written. They can add to that list as they pass by. When they come back to their own group they will consider the additional suggestions from the other groups.

When this process is finished the group should nominate representatives to work with you to put these proposals into improved policies, procedures and practices. This will take time, but the staff will be more committed when they can see that their efforts are being recognised and at least some of their ideas are being implemented. Time spent here will reduce the negative time spent later cleaning up problems.

■ CLARIFY POLICIES AND PROCEDURES

Problem-solving and conflict resolution is more likely to lead to positive outcomes in organisations that have clear guidelines, policies and procedures that are communicated effectively to all staff.

The best managers ensure that there are clear guidelines that are communicated to staff at the time of recruitment, at staff meetings, in training programs and in other support programs. They try to involve the staff in the development of their policies and procedures and encourage staff participation in their ongoing evaluation and modification. They know that the final accountability for implementation is theirs but they also know that there will be a higher level of commitment by the staff towards the success of the programs if they are directly involved in their design and any modifications to that design.

The best managers know that they can have greater flexibility in choosing options if they have a good solid base of policy construction. To them, policies and procedures are guidelines, not coercive directives or immutable laws punctuated by sanctions and penalties. These guidelines are a means to an end and not an end in themselves. Without this solid base, flexibility becomes chaos, ambiguity and confusion that in turn is more likely to lead to further conflicts. Compare doing a triple somersault with full twist from a good trampoline as against the same exercise from a soft beanbag.

Start with the policies, guidelines, priorities and procedures of the whole organisation. If they do not exist or are inadequate, take a leading role in coordinating a team to prepare or revise them. Then translate those goals and directions into your particular area of responsibility. Even when the general guidelines are inadequate there is no reason not to have effective ones in your unit. Target those areas in which conflict and disputes are more likely to occur; try to establish best practice in those areas and set up the mechanisms for dealing with conflict and its resolution.

Look specifically at factors such as:
- effective communication
- selection and recruitment
- induction
- working conditions
- promotion and succession planning
- performance development and appraisal
- feedback and reporting
- recognition and reward schemes
- training and development opportunities
- industrial or employee relations
- anti-discrimination
- cultural diversity
- equal employment opportunity
- sexual harassment
- counselling
- grievance procedures
- mediation and conciliation
- occupational health and safety
- rehabilitation programs
- joint consultative committees
- disciplinary and dismissal procedures.

Effective communication is the key to managing conflict. How effective are you as a communicator? Take confidence in those factors that indicate a real strength. Identify those areas that require further development, involvement and experience. Where can you get that support? Who can assist you in that area? It is important for us as leaders to set up programs to ensure that each and every staff member has access to the information required to participate on equal terms with everyone else and to have the guidelines required to perform their roles and responsibilities. Top operators not only make information available but also ensure that all staff members understand the messages. They timetable meetings to allow staff to have access to that knowledge and understanding and, through good questioning, they test their understanding of it.

■ FOLLOW BEST PRACTICE

It is difficult to define 'best practice' in a few words, but it is very easy to recognise it when you see it. Most organisations have a few people who get things done in a manner that gives the staff confidence to move forward in a cohesive, productive unit in which job satisfaction, cooperation and development are high priorities. Find leaders with these qualities and analyse what they do well and why they achieve a positive working environment. Why do staff want to work in their areas? Look at what they are doing in relation to the following.

HAVE EFFECTIVE TRAINING AND DEVELOPMENT PROGRAMS

The best organisations build in training programs as a regular part of staff development and progress, and recognise that the expenditure on such programs is more than compensated by the reduced costs in conflict management at a later date, as well as the improved productivity and outcomes that will flow from them. These organisations see that their highest priority is people management and client and customer service.

In order to improve the working environment and to improve dispute handling and conflict resolution, the best organisations include the following as a regular part of their development timetables:
- effective communication skills
- selection procedures
- recruitment and induction
- performance appraisal
- leadership
- supervision skills
- people management
- conflict resolution
- team building
- customer service

- dealing with difficult people
- negotiation and mediation skills
- problem-solving
- discrimination and equal employment opportunity
- occupational health and safety
- understanding industrial and employee relations.

IMPROVE RECRUITMENT AND INDUCTION

Too often, organisations recruit staff through various contacts or referrals, or through a process of simple advertising followed by the review of a one- or two-page résumé and a quick interview aimed at an evaluation of the person's technical and professional skills and qualifications. These initial selection processes have shortcomings and people are often selected for the wrong reasons and are therefore misplaced. Misplaced people are unhappy and unfulfilled and this leads them into conflicts.

Companies that recruit with reference only to skills, qualifications and experience often have a high incidence of conflict and disputes. There is often a high level of leave applications and a disproportionate staff turnover and resignation rate. They are more likely to be faced by claims of unfair dismissal. Consider the ongoing costs of these factors against the establishment of effective selection and induction processes. While the majority of staff will adjust and become effective people in the workplace, those who lack the necessary people skills will constitute a disproportionate burden for the supervisor or manager because of their inability to work as part of the team. They will create or become involved in conflict situations and increase the workload of others.

Those organisations that are more serious about the selection of the right people for the job, with an emphasis on people skills, will be looking for staff who will contribute to the team effort and will have the flexibility and adaptability to meet the ever-changing needs of the group. As a first priority, clarify the roles and responsibilities of the position to be filled and the remuneration to be paid. Identify the qualifications and experience required by that person to be eligible for further consideration. In the job description, advertisement and during the interview, identify and evaluate those important people qualities that you require in the person for them to be an effective team member and for them to contribute to the quality outcomes. What type of person do you want in your organisation? If you don't get the people part right first, then all of the other qualifications and experience will not flow through effectively to the organisation.

The recruitment process should be given this emphasis because we are trying to create a working environment in which conflicts are less likely to occur and, when they do, they will be managed quickly and effectively through a cooperative effort of the team. To support the selection of the most appropriate person, ensure that there are induction programs in place. Remember that the new recruit has not been to the numerous staff meetings at which you have cast your pearls of wisdom to the masses. Nor have they attended development programs or been part of working parties that have helped to develop policies and guidelines for the group.

ESTABLISH MENTOR PROGRAMS

Mentor programs are established to link people with greater knowledge, skills, experience and understanding to other staff members so that the less experienced can benefit from the guidance of the more experienced. Mentor programs are far less threatening than a normal supervisor/supervised relationship. These programs break down the isolation and insecurity that many members of staff feel. Mentor programs encourage people to discuss issues of concern before they develop into major crises. They improve the openness and honesty in communications and they create an atmosphere in which people work side by side to resolve problems together.

In addition to the obvious benefits to the person receiving the guidance, the program also benefits the mentor. When a mentor aspires to take on further leadership roles, the experience of mentoring will provide great experience in managing people in a positive manner. It will enhance their understanding of performance evaluation, program design, skills auditing, planning, performance development and reporting of effective outcomes. It will make them more aware of the impact that guidance and development can have on the individual and the organisation. They will be more aware of the environment in which conflict is likely to occur and be in a better position to deal with it early, should it begin to emerge. Mentors develop those important people management skills so essential to the management of conflict in higher positions.

TRAIN SELECTION COMMITTEES

The selection of the wrong person to a position has the potential to cause disharmony in the team and lead to conflict and disputes. This will add to negative outcomes and an increased emphasis on dealing with problems in the organisation. So, the selection of the right person for the job at any level is crucial to the total effect of the team. It is important therefore to train all supervisors and managers in selection techniques, how to prepare role statements, how to prepare advertisements, how to select the appropriate criteria and organise information packages about the job.

A clear understanding of the provisions of anti-discrimination legislation and the principles and practices surrounding equal employment opportunity are essential to anyone involved in the selection process. It can be an advantage to have an independent person — say, from another section — on a selection panel to act as a moderator against bias or unacceptable behaviour in the process. Be conscious of the need to give unbiased consideration to those from minority groups and those who are disadvantaged.

PRACTISE COUNSELLING

On many occasions in the workplace you will be approached by people in difficult situations, wishing to seek advice and counselling. The best people managers are those who take on this role effectively. These will be the occasions when you can effectively manage conflicts or disputes at the place where they occur. Promote the idea to staff that you are available for counselling and give them the confidence that, should you not be able to assist, you will be able to direct them to other sources of counselling within the organisation or from government or community agencies.

Identify people in the organisation who might be able to assist you when required. There might be specialists or experienced people in the Human Resources section. Specialists in government agencies such as the Health Department might be able to assist when the situation goes beyond your skills and training.

PROMOTE AND PRACTISE MEDIATION AND CONCILIATION

Promote the concept and practise of mediation and conciliation in the workplace, especially on an informal basis. Make yourself available to act as a mediator in disputes. Identify other people in the organisation or from outside who could act as an independent mediator in alternative dispute resolution procedures. Include mediation in your development programs so that staff become fully aware of the processes and benefits to all concerned.

APPOINT CONTACT PERSONS

Conflicts and disputes often develop because people are afraid to go to a supervisor or manager to complain. They fear that it might reflect badly on them if they lodge a complaint. Those same people are more likely to air their grievance to another member of staff. To ensure that matters of concern are brought to light early and acted on quickly it is best to provide an avenue for people to air any grievances. Ask the staff to elect one or two people who are highly respected by all staff, are experienced and have the necessary personal qualities to be a contact person to whom others can go to discuss matters of concern. These people become a vital link between staff, and you should give them your support and guidance.

ESTABLISH EFFECTIVE GRIEVANCE PROCEDURES

Grievance procedures are often looked upon in a negative light because they are seen as just another avenue for people to air their complaints against the management. Some supervisors or managers do not like dealing with complaints and will take the option of avoidance if possible until the situation becomes so critical that they have to act in order to prevent — or to control — a real crisis. At that stage the conflict is more difficult to control, will usually result in negative penalties and sanctions and will be more costly in time, effort and emotional stress.

There are a number of reasons why grievance procedures fail. In setting up your own procedures, there are a number of pitfalls that should be avoided. These include:

- The reasons are not outlined for the decision.
- The decisions appear to be inconsistent.
- The procedures are conducted in an area that is too remote from the parties involved.
- There is a lack of trust and confidence in other parties.
- The parties losing sight of the real issues.
- The issues may be clouded in emotion.
- There are too many hidden agendas.
- There are budget restraints.
- Other tasks and functions assume a higher 'importance'.
- The rules and regulations are inflexible.
- The opportunity for promotion might act as a caution.
- There is a fear of failure.
- The procedures are not understood.
- Individuals may not be comfortable with procedures.
- Some people are not emotionally suited to negotiations.
- Managers like to make decisions, not waste time negotiating.
- There may be a fear by managers that equity and equal employment opportunities for others reduces their own status and influence.
- There is a lack of delegation of authority to make real decisions.
- The negotiator's not in a position to make decisions.
- Managers too often see a need to support supervisors regardless of what staff members say.
- There is philosophical opposition to the other side.
- There may be ambiguity and confusion as to the reason for the meeting.
- There may be inadequate research and attention to detailed facts.
- A poor attitude to the organisation and its management may exist.
- There is a perceived threat to a person's position.
- There is a lack of experience and training in this area.

It is important to establish grievance procedures that are open, transparent and known by all staff. Take the opportunity during staff meetings and training programs to emphasise the importance of the procedures and their prime focus on providing an environment in which people can work together towards resolving disputes and solving problems. Emphasise the positive outcomes that will emanate from them rather than the negative aspects of the conflict.

Assure the staff that differences in approach and the conflicts and disputes that come from them are inevitable in the workplace but, if managed correctly, they can result in real progress. Break down the traditional attitude of 'them and us'. Develop the culture that accepts that problems and mistakes occur even in the best organisations, but are best resolved by everyone working together. In this environment, grievance procedures are more of a cooperative effort towards improvement rather than a hot spot of negative criticism.

In setting up grievance procedures consider the following:

The number of steps
- some organisations have specific procedures
- keep the process simple.

Who will be involved?
- first involve those as close as possible to the dispute
- involve the supervisor and union delegate
- have participants resolve the issues if possible
- keep it in-house if possible
- outline implications if not settled in-house.

What is to be negotiated?
- clarify the level, stage and seriousness of the dispute or grievance
- clarify levels of authority and decision making
- what issues are to be included and which excluded?

What is the time frame?
- outline benefits of handling the matter quickly
- determine the benefits of taking time to resolve
- propose a time line as a starting point.

Options for outcomes
- propose and analyse a range of options
- have them brainstorm various options
- outline benefits of coming to agreement
- possibility of penalties or sanctions in serious cases
- types of penalties or sanctions.

What happens while the dispute is in progress?
- what conditions apply?
- do you maintain current conditions?
- are wages affected?
- are safety issues involved?

Follow-up to the process
- action to take place
- what support will be given?

- who will be involved?
- the time line for implementation
- monitoring and evaluation.

Most grievances can be handled on an informal basis within the unit. Some might require the involvement of representatives from human resources or from senior management. The most serious cases require a more formal procedure and this is when the structured processes come into effect. The other situation when grievance procedures come into effect is when there have been disputes or conflicts regarding formal awards or contracts of employment. In those situations, unions and/or legal representatives might be involved. It is best, however, to deal with these matters in-house early in the dispute rather than allow them to develop to a point where they are taken out of your hands and decided in the Industrial Commission or a court.

ELIMINATE DISCRIMINATORY PRACTICES

If someone believes that they are being treated unfairly they will not perform to their potential, and the resulting loss of productivity and effectiveness is a loss to the organisation and a potential increase in disputes. Conflict occurs mostly because people are different, not necessarily because they are wrong. Discrimination and sexual harassment are against state, provincial and national laws in most countries. The combined effect of these laws means that it is unlawful to treat employees unfairly or to limit their opportunities on the basis of gender, pregnancy, race, colour, ethnic background, religion, marital status, sexuality, age or disability.

Discrimination might be direct or indirect. It is direct discrimination when actions and decisions are based on traditional views of gender, age, race, etc. It is indirect when there are policies, rules, guidelines or unwritten practices that restrict access to certain groups. For example, a warehouse person is 'required to be able to lift 80 kilograms (180 pounds)'; 'Only people who can speak fluent English can be employed'; 'Security officers must be at least 180 centimetres (6 feet) tall'. A job advertisement that indicates that only candidates in the age bracket 25 to 35 will be considered is discriminatory; as is the policy that during a restructuring, married women and part-time employees will be made redundant first.

The first principle of any employment or selection process is to do it on the basis of merit, that is the best person gets the position provided that each and every applicant has equal access to apply and be considered.

In considering people with disabilities it is reasonable to make adjustments in consideration of that disability. For example, a person in a wheelchair might be allowed to work on the ground floor so that they have easy access to the building and to toilets for the disabled. Consideration is given to disabled persons above the ground floor in the event of a fire, when they would have to be taken down stairs.

Equal employment opportunity (EEO) is merely the reverse of discrimination. It ensures that each and every person has an equal opportunity to be considered for positions and to be treated fairly. Ensure that all persons involved in recruitment and selection are conversant with the legislation and the policies and procedures relating to discrimination and EEO. That legislation ensures that employers are legally liable for breaches in the areas of discrimination and harassment when it happens at work or in the context of work. So it is important for you to take an active role in managing this crucial aspect of human resources.

As a supervisor or manager you represent the employer and the organisation and therefore take responsibility for this area within your span of control. It is a crucial area that cannot be passed on to other managers or to the Human Resources section. While you might seek their guidance and support, it is you who will carry the responsibility for the effective implementation of EEO and for any outcomes from its mismanagement. You are advised to set up programs that deal with these issues.

You will provide the necessary training and development to all staff to raise their levels of awareness and understanding of these issues and the procedures to be adopted when there is a breach or when there is a complaint. A working environment should be developed in which discrimination and harassment is less likely to occur. Try to anticipate the situations that have the potential for discrimination or harassment to occur and make the necessary adjustments to forestall them. Deal with complaints expeditiously and effectively and with confidence

The procedures to deal with complaints must be accessible to and known by all. Give consideration to groups or individuals who have been discriminated against in the past. Make reasonable adjustments for people with disabilities. Look to different arrangements to accommodate differences and to get the best from each member of staff. Ensure that selection procedures take EEO principles into consideration. Give instructions in a form or in languages that can be understood by all staff. Test the staff's understanding of policies and instructions especially when they relate to safety. Avoid asking for personal details that do not relate to the job. Be consistent from person to person, time to time and place to place.

PREVENT HARASSMENT

Does your organisation have a policy regarding a good working environment? If there is no specific policy you might be able to assist in coordinating a representative group to construct such a policy.

To assist you in this process contact your nearest anti-discrimination authority. They will have ample documentation and guidelines on these matters and will often be available to meet with you and the staff to clarify meanings, discuss case studies and assist in developing policies and good practice. These authorities place a high priority on education to prevent discrimination. They would rather take that approach than dealing out penalties and sanctions after the event.

Harassment is any form of behaviour that is not wanted, not asked for and not encouraged. Behaviour that causes hostility, humiliation, serious embarrassment, offence or intimidation is harassment. Such matters as the distribution of racist, sexist or homophobic material; verbal abuse or comments; sexual behaviour; rude or stereotyped jokes or excessive initiation rites are unacceptable. These things are the cause of much conflict in the workplace and so must be addressed by you as a regular part of your people management. The more serious cases occur when there is a distinct difference in relative power or authority or influence between the two people. While the action might be intentional or unintentional, there is a general rule that if it causes embarrassment or if the other person feels uncomfortable, then it is unacceptable.

To prevent harassment:

- Develop a policy for 'good working relations'.
- Set an exemplary standard in your own behaviour.
- Ensure that the staff have copies of the policy and any related material such as legislation and guidelines.
- Include these matters in staff meetings and development programs.
- Ensure that staff know how to deal with harassment when it happens to them.
- Be prepared to answer those who see this as a trivial waste of time.
- Remove material that staff believe is harassing.
- Stamp out practices, such as initiation rites, that are unacceptable, no matter how long it has been a common practice in the organisation.
- Follow up on indicators of staff behaviours that might indicate a problem.
- As staff might be embarrassed in discussing these issues with management, it is advisable to appoint a well respected staff member as a contact person to whom others can go, as a first point of call, to get advice in a confidential manner.
- Ensure that the organisation has a grievance procedure to deal with complaints or allegations.
- Follow your organisation's grievance procedure.
- Act immediately in dealing with complaints.
- Treat each complaint seriously and show sensitivity and empathy.
- Gather all of the information from the complainant.
- Question whether you are the appropriate person to deal with the complaint.
- Act fairly, impartially and honestly in handling these cases.
- Put the allegation to the other person and give them time to respond.
- Decide whether you should interview other people to clarify details.
- Distinguish whether it is a relatively minor matter that can be handled by mediation or conciliation on the shop floor, or a more serious case that will require more serious disciplinary procedures or criminal proceedings.
- Make it clear to all concerned what action you will take and how each person is to be involved in those proceedings.
- Monitor the outcomes.

ESTABLISH DISCIPLINARY PROCEDURES

When a situation reaches the stage where a staff member has to be disciplined, ensure that the basic principles of natural justice, presumed innocence, fairness and honesty are implemented.

Disciplinary action can vary from simple cautions and reprimands to very serious matters leading to possible dismissal or criminal charges.

Most countries' industrial legislation provides for cases of unfair dismissal, and the publicity surrounding these cases has made management in many organisations reticent to act against employees who are causing problems. Be confident that you can establish procedures to deal with serious disciplinary matters provided that the following points are taken into consideration:

- The actions taken by the management are not harsh, unjust or unreasonable.
- The procedures are fair to all concerned.
- The employee is notified of the concerns and is given an opportunity to respond to them.
- The employee is given ample warning of the concerns and sufficient support and time to correct those concerns.
- The employee is given the opportunity to obtain further advice.
- There is a valid reason for the dismissal based on the employee's incapacity to work or their improper conduct.
- A plan of development and support is implemented.
- Illness or injury is not a reason for dismissal.
- Union membership or activities are not valid reasons for dismissal.
- Matters covered by discrimination legislation are not used as reasons for dismissal.
- Sufficient notice or pay in lieu of notice is given.
- Approved leave is not used as an opportunity to dismiss.

Underlying all of these matters is the principle of a fair go for all concerned. If you have clear guidelines and good work practices, with ongoing monitoring and support, no employee should be in a situation where the threat of a dismissal is a surprise to them. If your staff development program is open, honest, supportive and well documented, with copies given to each person then you can proceed with confidence should the need arise to discipline or dismiss an employee.

DEAL WITH UNION REPRESENTATIVES

If your staff belong to a union I advise you to make contact with the local organiser and set up open lines of communication with that person. No organisation is perfect and there will always be conflicts and disputes that arise. These need to be brought to your attention for action. Mistakes are made and the sooner they are corrected the better for all concerned. I have found from experience that the closer to the place of work that the problem is addressed the more effective will be the outcome and the greater confidence the staff will have in your management.

In the perfect world staff will come to you with concerns and you, in turn, will deal with the matter expeditiously and positively for the benefit of all. But this is not a perfect world and unions are there to ensure that the workers' rights are met and complaints are dealt with. Through their collective weight they provide a balance to the power and authority of the organisation. The best way to guarantee a balance and a good working relationship is to work together in a joint problem-solving approach with the union representative.

Over the years I have learnt from experience to encourage staff to have a union representative or colleague present at meetings involving serious allegations or at any follow-up disciplinary meetings. These people are innocent until proven guilty and they have the right to have support and advice during the process. Your advice and encouragement in this regard will show your fairness and independence and will assist your management of the complaints. The local union organiser likes to work at their level where they are seen to be having an influence and it is an advantage to give them credit and recognition for bringing real issues to your attention. It is much easier to deal with a problem in the early stages at the local level than later on in a distant formal court or tribunal where you do not have control or influence.

ESTABLISH OHS COMMITTEES

Occupational health and safety (OHS) is an area where conflicts and complaints occur very often in the workplace. The time lost in industry caused by occupational injuries and sickness on average would be 10 to 20 times more than that caused by industrial action. Check with the HR and finance sections to calculate the cost of workers' compensation, leave provisions, insurance premiums, rehabilitation, legal and other costs involved in workplace injuries and illness. These costs are magnified in industries where there is a majority of workers from a non-English speaking background who tend to work in poorly paid jobs in high-risk industries such as process workers in factories and labourers in the building and construction fields.

Your first priority is to make yourself conversant with current legislation in this area. Do it yourself because ignorance of these provisions will not be an excuse if a major crisis occurs. Make contact with the government authority that is responsible for this area because they will have lots of publications, most of which are free, that are written in everyday language that is easily understood and can be easily implemented. They will often conduct training programs at their centres or at your place of work. Program OHS into your everyday management using the advice from these authorities. At the very least, I suggest that the following strategies should be included in your plan:
- Establish an occupational health and safety committee as a cooperative team of both management and workers.
- Select key contact people to whom workers can go with concerns and ensure that everyone knows who they are.

- Ensure that all signs are in simple English and, when necessary, use multilingual signs.
- Have a representative from a non-English background on the OHS committee.
- Promote the concept of OHS at staff meetings, in training programs and in newsletters.
- Show that you and other supervisors and managers act quickly on matters raised.
- Ensure that supervisors and staff are made aware of their responsibilities in regard to OHS.
- Ensure that supervisors are committed to and accountable for a safe working environment.
- Delegate authority to act in cases of unsafe conditions.
- Check that new equipment meets the standards required.
- Include OHS in your induction programs.
- Assure workers that it is helpful to identify and report problems.
- Encourage staff to complete first aid courses.

The planned thoughtful setting up of positive programs in the workplace will create an environment in which conflict is unlikely to occur. If it does, it will be possible to manage it quickly and concertedly. By involving the staff in this process you will be creating a safer, happier and more productive workplace.

Chapter 5 will take you through a number of practical exercises and activities that will assist you to assess your abilities and preparedness to manage conflict. It will also help you to prepare yourself and the organisation to change the direction and take on a more positive approach to conflict management.

Activities to help you build your conflict resolution skills

- Effective leadership
- Communication strategies
- Reacting well under pressure
- Towards a collaborative working environment

■ INTRODUCTION

If we are to be successful in managing conflicts something must happen to change the current situation. We established earlier in the book that it is virtually impossible to change the world; extremely difficult to change the organisations in which we live and work and very difficult to change other people's behaviour. So, if we are to improve our handling of conflict in the workplace, we will have to change our managerial approach.

To assist you through that change process, I have designed a number of exercises that I have found very useful both in the workplace and in the numerous training and development programs I have conducted over many years. In the first instance the emphasis is on self-analysis. We get so tied down at work with tasks, functions, processes, product and deadlines that we rarely take the time to analyse ourselves. Too rarely do we reflect on what we are doing well or what we need to develop further in order to improve the people management skills so necessary for the better handling of conflict.

Identify your strengths, go with your strengths, use them with confidence and don't be ashamed to promote them.

The second purpose of these exercises is to identify those areas that require more development. Don't look on these as weaknesses but as aspects of your work that could be improved as part of your ongoing development. It is not a case of 'Yes, I have it' or 'No, I don't'. It is a matter of the stage of development you have reached in each area — I can do word processing but it is an area where I need much more experience and development. When you have identified these items try to include them in your annual program of development. When you have done your self-analysis you will find that you have many more attributes and skills than you first thought and this will give you the confidence to be more involved in the handling of disputes.

Other exercises in this chapter relate to your reactions in critical situations, your ability to communicate effectively during those crises, the manner in which you relate to the people with whom you work and the strategies for handling conflicts and difficult people. When you have completed the main activities, I suggest that you then sit down and determine what you will change in order to be a more effective person in handling conflict resolution and disputes.

activity **1** am I an effective leader, supervisor or manager of people in critical situations?

Over the last 25 years I have conducted hundreds of development programs which have included aspects of good leadership, management or supervision in the context of handling conflicts, disputes and difficult people. During those programs I have asked the numerous participants to identify those special qualities that they regard as essential or desirable in a good leader, manager or supervisor. Each group surveyed produced an almost identical list of qualities. There were, of course, some variations in number and type, but there was a general consistency in what people wanted in a good leader. Those characteristics are listed below. There is no priority in the order listed.

Look at the list below and consider first whether or not you consider that these are the qualities that you would like in someone who leads, directs or supervises you and your work. If so, then you must measure yourself against this list to test your own effectiveness as a leader or supervisor responsible for other workers. Others will be looking for these same qualities in you.

Tick those characteristics that are your real strengths and circle those that require more development.

- Striving for excellence.
- Having vitality.
- Making the tough decisions.
- Working well under pressure.
- Having knowledge and awareness.
- Being practical and realistic.
- Setting goals and outcomes.
- Having the courage of their convictions.
- Looking for better ways of doing things.
- Being a good communicator.
- Inspiring s others.
- Testing and monitoring progress.
- Taking action to prevent problems.
- Providing developmental feedback.
- Being able to motivate employees.
- Being a self-starter.
- Having respect of staff, clients and customers.
- Willingness to admit errors.
- Able to analyse and report accurately.
- Being honest and open.
- Being fair and equitable

- Willing to take the lead.
- Being intuitive.
- Accepting responsibility.
- Handling crises.
- Having vision.
- Having demonstrated skills and experience.
- Understanding policies and legislation.
- Having strength of purpose.
- Having a balanced perspective.
- Being a good listener.
- Willing to delegate with confidence.
- Possessing analytical skills.
- Recognising and rewarding excellence.
- Showing initiative.
- Being confident.
- Being a positive thinker.
- Possessing integrity and tact.
- Having the courage to change if necessary.
- Working well with people.
- Being approachable.
- Having imagination.

- Showing compassion.
- Listening to other opinions.
- Being cooperative.
- Enhancing their own development.
- Being a good negotiator and mediator.
- Able to organise and coordinate.
- Having a sense of humour.
- Sustaining energy.
- Able to rise above the situation.
- Being sensitive to others.
- Exercising patience.
- Being flexible and adaptable.
- Encouraging others to develop.
- Planning effectively.
- Having charisma; being personable.
- Providing cohesion to the team.
- Enjoying good health.
- Being intelligent and able to think smart.

activity 2 — how easily can I handle pressure and deal with crises?

In an ideal world we would all work happily together in a comfortable environment without pressure, crises or unreasonable demands. But this is not an ideal world. The real world is one of constant change, confusion, ambiguity, grievance, anxiety and one in which we are constantly confronted by pressure, demands and crises. How well are you able to meet these demands?

Look at the following list. Tick those points that you consider are your strengths and circle those needing development.

- I plan ahead.
- I deal with problems quickly and fairly.
- I have good reasoning powers.
- I remain calm under pressure.
- People look to me for action and guidance.
- I easily assume control in difficult situations.
- I seek cooperation of others.
- I establish clear priorities.
- I can coordinate people.
- I give clear directions.
- I work easily in a team.
- I monitor the progress of my actions.
- I have the courage to act under pressure.
- I am confident in dealing with difficult people.
- I am effective in the bargaining process.
- I am an effective mediator.
- I am prepared to consider options.
- I can act with compassion and sensitivity.
- I am punctual.
- I can analyse situations clearly.
- I anticipate problems before they happen.
- I provide comfort for those under stress.
- I move quickly to assess damage or injury.
- I identify and co-opt key people in a crisis.
- I am an effective communicator.
- I communicate a plan of action.
- I can identify available resources.
- I can allocate tasks.
- I take responsibility for my actions.
- I establish clear reporting procedures.
- I am willing to take risks.
- I have good interviewing skills.
- I have good negotiation skills.
- I establish grievance resolution procedures.
- I quickly clarify an authority to act.
- I evaluate effectiveness after the event.

Look at the following list. Tick those points that you consider are your strengths and circle those needing development.

- I check that others understand my messages.
- I use many ways of getting my message across.
- My tone of voice and my body language is consistent with my verbal message.
- I express my feelings appropriately.
- I share my ideas assertively.
- I participate freely in discussions and meetings.
- I admit responsibility for my actions.
- I ask others for their ideas and contributions.
- I am willing to listen to the opinions of others.
- I respect the rights of others to hold opinions even when they differ from mine.
- I try to understand the goals, concerns and needs of others.
- I try to gain commitment from others.
- I am open and honest in my dealings with others.
- I allow the other person to finish without interruption.
- I provide open and honest feedback
- I acknowledge others for their good work.
- I try not to make assumptions about the other person's background or personality.
- I try not to make assumptions about what the other person might say.
- I respect other people's cultures and values even when they differ from mine.
- I seek to clarify each point or issue.
- I test my understanding of what has been said.
- I ask clarifying questions.
- I contribute to policies and procedures.
- I handle conflict calmly.
- I try to help others in crisis situations.
- I attack issues and not the person.
- I spend time considering issues.
- I am flexible and willing to change.
- I can think through issues and prepare follow-up actions.
- I stick to the facts, not hearsay and opinion.
- I reformulate for the other person what I understand them to have said.
- I allow for silence, space and time.

Look at the second list and repeat the exercise.

use my reasoning skills.

research and analyse the situation.

look for opportunities for improvement.

propose and assess a range of options.

utilise the expertise of the other people.

try to understand the fears and concerns of others.

put myself in their position.

respect the others and understand the direction from which they come.

recognise the responsibility and accountability of others.

pay respect to a person's authority.

work together towards solving the problem.

try to negotiate in the early stages.

promote cooperation, collaboration and active participation.

use my knowledge, skills and experience to guide others.

act as a mediator to assist others in a dispute situation.

use friendliness as a means to cooperation.

value the contributions of the people involved in the dispute.

put all of the information on the table.

work together to clarify the issues and canvass the options for agreement.

Look at the following list. Tick those points that you consider are your strengths and circle those needing development.

- Being intelligent.
- Having knowledge of the subject being disputed.
- Possessing good reasoning skills.
- Thinking in logical patterns.
- Restoring order from chaos.
- Conceptualising things in sequential patterns.
- Being analytical.
- Able to research.
- Having planning skills.
- Thinking ahead of the action.
- Being aware of time demands.
- Having 180- to 360-degree vision.
- Able to solve problems.
- Controlling emotions.
- Bargaining.
- Being prepared.

- Focusing on issues.
- Thinking clearly.
- Working well under pressure.
- Being articulate.
- Willing to share information.
- Willing to assist others in a crisis.
- Possessing good questioning and listening skills.
- Having integrity.
- Showing empathy.
- Respecting the pressures on others.
- Being persuasive and persistent.
- Being determined and decisive.
- Willing to take risks.
- Being flexible and adaptable.
- Having confidence and courage.
- Able to handle crises.
- Willing to consider a range of options.

activity 5 — what are the indicators of conflict in your workplace?

As you walk around your area of responsibility be aware of the indicators of conflict, and anticipate the likely outcomes should they be not be addressed. Look for incidents that might reflect that all is not well. Good referees in sport will often give advice and direction on the run when they first see a situation developing, rather than waiting for it to develop further. They do this before having to apply harsh penalties or reach the stage when they lose control of the game and the respect of the players. The best referees have a 180-degree span of vision and are very good at anticipating what is likely to happen next. They move in calmly and confidently to manage the situations before they develop. The best managers act in the same way.

Look now to the following as indicators of concern. To what extent and in what circumstances do these occur in your workplace? Can you add to that list?

Conflict indicators

Stress	Anger
Aggression	Poor performance
Increased sick leave	Threat of resignation
Applications for transfer	Emotional outbursts
Obvious discomfort	Difficulty in making decisions
Reticence to take responsibility	Separation
Aloofness	Ambiguity
Confusion	Increased blood pressure
Flash points	Power plays
Raised voices	Tension
Increased criticisms	Sarcasm and cynicism
Walkouts	Tantrums and tears
Misunderstandings	Reticence to talk about issues
Lack of commitment	Mistrust
Retreat from situations	Siege mentality
Physical and verbal abuse	Harassment
Resignation rates	Resentment
Fear	Hurt
Guilt	Blaming
Retaliation	Blackmail

activity 6 — how often do I react neg[...] in difficult situations?

How do you normally react in difficult situations? To what extent do yo[...] listed below? The list identifies reactions that fall into confrontationist c[...] punch them or run away; or head butt and scare them off patterns. If w[...] we will admit that we have all used most or all of these behaviours at [...]

First, think of those occasions when you adopted that confront[...] circumstances under which it happened. If you were in that situa[...] change your approach? Secondly, tick the items that you tend[...] management. How effective have they been in the short and long te[...] have approached the situation differently? What will you do to cha[...]

- I have violent outbursts to gain attention or frighten others a[...]
- I use penalties or sanctions to punish the perpetrators.
- I constantly interrupt the other person.
- I use sarcasm or cynicism to establish my superiority.
- I use insulting terms to get my message across.
- I look for opportunities to score points in order to gain con[...]
- I use my intellect to belittle the other person.
- I preach and moralise to establish my higher values.
- I talk over the other person to get them back to my point[...]
- I demand that I am right and that there are no alternative[...]
- I use threats, blackmail and ultimatums.
- I use laws, rules and regulations to explain my actions or[...]
- I withhold or selectively release information.
- I emphasise my status or position to establish credibility.[...]
- I limit or suppress discussion because it takes valuable t[...]
- I refuse or limit access to materials.
- I look for opportunities to get even.
- I walk out and refuse to participate.
- I am highly critical of others.
- I avoid taking responsibility.
- I blame others and try to make them feel guilty.
- I try to distract them by being super-nice.
- I attempt to trivialise the issue so that it does not war[...]
- I put the matter aside and hope it will go away.

activity **8** *moving from reaction to action*

It is important to transmit your feelings and emotions in such a manner that others can understand how you are reacting to the situation. It is also important to read your own feelings and to try to understand them. This activity will assist you to prepare for what has to happen and the direction you will take. Think of a conflict in which you have been involved or one that you have observed; look past the reactions and emotions and then answer the following questions.

- What is the nature of the problem?
- Are you focused on the issue and not on the person?
- To what extent are you involved in that situation?
- Are you focused on the present and not on the past?
- Who else is part of the problem?
- Where and from whom will you get support and guidance?
- Do you know what to say?
- Have you clarified the extent to which you want to communicate emotions to others?
- With whom should you communicate and why?
- When and how should you release the tension and stress?
- How will you look for more positive outcomes?
- Who should be part of the solution and resolution?
- How will you improve relationships that might have been affected by the current situation?

Look to your own communication style and that of others who work with you. What can you do to limit or eradicate the problems with the messenger that might cause or aggravate conflicts? Consider the following points. One, some or many of these may relate to the messenger. Put yourself in the messenger's shoes.

- The person transmitting the message might be unsure of what should be communicated.
- They may be uncertain about the issues, idea or proposal.
- There may be a lack of understanding of the mission, vision, goals, priorities and expected outcomes.
- The messenger may have only limited access to information.
- They may have inadequate time and resources to prepare the message, which could result in a confusing message.
- They may have preconceived ideas of the other person.
- They lack commitment to the message, the audience or the organisation.
- They may have a poor attitude to the organisation.
- They may be suffering from low self-esteem, lack of confidence or courage.
- They may lack clarity in their own beliefs.
- There may be inconsistency from person to person, time to time and place to place, which kills the confidence and trust that the receiver has in the messenger and the message.
- They may take a reactive stance such as aggression, defensiveness, superiority, coercion, ridicule, sarcasm or cynicism.
- They may have unreal expectations.
- They may use different channels for communication.
- They may deliberately set out to confuse in order to show their perceived superiority or to distract attention from the real issue.

Messages can be distorted by a number of factors. How often and in what circumstances have you used these tactics to distract someone from getting their message across? How did it affect your attempts to resolve the dispute? How can you improve in this regard?

- Noise: raising your voice and shouting certainly gains attention but will often distort the message and make it more difficult to reach agreement.
- Denying any involvement or responsibility.
- Appearing to be dealing with the matter but really working to hidden agendas.
- Distracting the messenger from their objective by using tantrums and tears.
- Blaming others: this is an attempt to transfer the problem to another person and therefore relieve the pressure on oneself.
- Insinuating or stating that the other person is guilty: this puts them on the defensive and shifts the focus of the agenda.
- Showing anger and aggression: this creates fear and the desire to run away or avoid the conflict.
- Praise: used to create a false sense of security.
- Constantly interrupting: this can be very frustrating.
- Creating fear.
- Using threats or blackmail.
- Running away or avoiding the situation.
- Employing strong power plays and the use of body language: these are used to distract and divert your attention.
- Manipulating others.
- Withholding information or giving misinformation.
- Criticising or physically attacking others.

How might you overcome the problems caused when your messages are not getting through to the intended audience? How will you address these issues in critical situations? Consider the following points.

- Being inattentive, which can be deliberate, a result of inadequate understanding or an incapacity to understand the message.
- Having a poor attitude to the messenger or source.
- Having inadequate confidence and self-esteem.
- Interrupting, which jolts the flow of communication.
- Being tuned to a different channel.
- Blaming a different language or culture.
- Having different values.
- Believing there is a perceived or real threat.
- Thinking something is beyond their level of experience and understanding.
- Using coercion, power plays and body language.
- Being aggressive.
- Being defensive.
- Having inadequate interest.
- Not being directly involved in the matter.
- Being inexperienced.
- Having a lack of knowledge of the area.
- Having poor skills.
- Being overworked.
- Having inadequate time to deal with the matter.
- Being unable to anticipate and analyse hidden agendas.
- Having misplaced faith in the messenger.

activity 12 *framing questions*

Questioning is one of the most important skills to be used in managing conflict resolution.

Good questioning can be used to control the emotion, direction and progress of a meeting or interview. Look to how the other party is behaving and design questions to bring the discussion back into focus. Use questions not statements. Use the following table as a guide. Assess the other person's behaviour and then design your question.

THE OTHER PERSON	YOUR QUESTION
Becomes very emotional and uses jumbled words and phrases.	E.g., Would you like me to repeat the last point and outline the reasons for it?
Stops speaking and becomes stressed.	E.g., Would you like a five-minute break?
Quickly changes the topic.	
Quickly skips over a number of topics.	
Says something that appears different from before.	
Keeps going over the same topic or accusations.	
Clouds the real issues with generalisations.	
Appears to be telling you what they think you want to hear.	
Moves into sensitive areas with possible legal implications.	
Suggests that this meeting is a waste of time.	
Won't accept an option that you have put forward.	
Does not want to be in the room with the other person in the conflict.	
Makes rude physical gestures.	
Has put forward an option or a number of options for action.	
Refuses to put forward an option, as it is not their problem.	
Has accused you of bias towards the other party.	
Accepts some points but strongly refutes the others.	
Will not accept your rewording of what they have said.	
Stands up, becomes agitated and wants to leave the room.	

The better you prepare for an interview, the more confidence you will have in conducting it and the more likely you will be able to deal with the fluctuations and emotions that will emerge and cloud the issues. Below are some questions you might ask yourself in preparation for an interview.

- Where will I conduct the interview?
- What must I do beforehand?
- Do I have the necessary information and facts?
- How will I introduce and welcome each person?
- Will I invite them to have representatives?
- How will I conduct the meeting?
- How will I introduce the topic?
- Have I clarified the role of the panel, the interviewee and any support persons?
- How will I structure the interview?
- Have I isolated the real issues?
- Have I given everyone a chance to be involved?
- Have I tested my understanding of the matters raised?
- Have I dealt with each issue in turn?
- Have I allowed for breaks?
- Have I encouraged a joint problem-solving approach?
- Have I managed the emotions and focused on the agenda?
- Am I striving towards agreement?
- Have I considered imbalances of power and influence?
- Have I avoided making assumptions?
- Have I shared time equitably?
- Have I provided the opportunity for each person to respond?
- Have we brainstormed a range of options and possible outcomes?
- Have I clarified what might happen if the matter remains unresolved?
- Am I prepared to make changes?
- Have I been flexible enough to incorporate their suggestions?
- Are we attempting to reach clear agreements?
- Does everyone have copies of all documents?
- Do we have a plan to follow-up and monitor the outcomes?

activity 14 — creating a preventative working environment

Look at your own area of responsibility and then at the total organisation in which you work and assess the extent to which a positive, cooperative and collaborative working environment has been developed to prevent or reduce the likelihood of conflicts occurring. Look to the extent that staff members are involved in real decision making and policy formulation. How far have you delegated responsibility?

Look at the following list. Tick those points that you consider are your strengths and circle those needing development.

- The organisation has clear goals and expected outcomes.
- Functions and tasks are well organised.
- Staff know what is expected of them.
- System coordination assists the flow of work.
- Organisational priorities are well understood.
- There is an openness and honesty.
- Staff members are trusted.
- There is a great deal of respect in the workplace.
- You are respected for what you can do.
- Personal needs are taken into consideration.
- People with problems can receive support.
- It is a good environment in which to work.
- Different cultures and values are respected.
- Staff members are confident to approach their supervisors.
- Staff members are treated fairly.
- Staff members trust their supervisors.
- People are encouraged to raise concerns.
- People with grievances are given a fair hearing.
- There is a group solution to problems.
- Disputes are resolved quickly and fairly.
- Team effort and achievement is rewarded.
- Individual effort and achievement is rewarded.
- People do notice what you do.
- There is very good feedback on performance.
- There is an expectation of quality performance.
- Team members help each other.
- Team members work together to solve problems.
- People identify with the team.

- There is a cooperative spirit.
- The team accepts responsibility as a unit.
- There is pride in the work of the group.
- People are allowed to make mistakes.
- Members change roles in the group.
- They work across teams.
- They are encouraged to participate in decisions.
- Each team is allocated adequate resources.
- There is cohesion within and between teams.
- Meetings are structured to involve staff.
- Staff is kept informed.
- Individuals understand what is happening and why.
- Communications are clear and understood.
- Staff members are trained in effective communication.
- There is a flow of information between teams.
- They understand what other units are doing and why.
- Information flows freely and clearly to other units.
- We all actively participate in meetings.
- Changes are thought out and well communicated.
- Each person is encouraged to try new approaches.
- Guidance, support and training are provided to all.
- People feel able to cope with the pressures of work.
- There are opportunities for professional development.
- Staff don't feel restricted by administrivia.
- Teams are given time to implement changes.
- People are encouraged to broaden their skills and experiences
- There is a feeling of camaraderie in the teams.
- Supervisors and managers are open to positive suggestions.
- Supervisors and managers are considered as part of teams.
- People enjoy working in teams.
- They are encouraged to make decisions at their level.

activity 15 | where do I stand between control and trust?

On the diagram below, mark the position that would best represent your general style of supervision or management, knowing that it will vary according to the situation. For example, if you are a very directive manager your position will be close to the vertical axis on the left. The classic example of a vertical model is the armed forces in which troops are expected to carry out orders without question or discussion. This approach is appropriate in times of war when rigid discipline is absolutely necessary. When the bullets are parting your hair there is no time to have a committee meeting. It is also appropriate in a crisis such as when a serious accident occurs and quick calm action and direction is necessary. If you are a very participatory type of manager your position will be closer to the right hand side of the spectrum.

Before marking your general position on the diagram consider the following:

- On the left side of the page list those factors of your responsibility that you believe must remain totally within your control.
- On the right side of the page list those factors for which your staff could take greater responsibility for and become more involved in real decision making. Include in that list all the things that you do on a day-to-day basis that could be successfully performed by a member of staff and thus be delegated.
- At the bottom of the page list those higher order leadership functions you could perform if you were released from the more routine tasks that you could now delegate.
- Then place an X on the diagonal of the diagram where you believe you generally operate on a day-to-day basis. Place a Y where you believe the staff would consider you to be. Place a Z where you would like to be.

FIGURE 5.1

The control–trust continuum

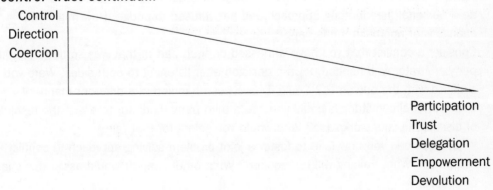

There are certain basic principles that underlie the need for greater participation of staff in the operations of the organisation and the degree of delegation, devolution of decision making and empowerment. Take the following points into consideration and then answer the questions that follow.

- People like to have a say in their own destiny.
- They will respond best when they believe that someone is listening and interested.
- Individuals like to have some control over their own affairs.
- Ownership brings with it a deeper sense of responsibility.
- Participants will invest more into something in which they have ownership.
- The ideas of those directly involved have value and can add to further development.
- Individuals are more protective of territory over which they feel they have control.
- An invitation to participate must be genuine, not tokenism.
- The project at hand must warrant the time and effort to be involved.
- The expected or desired outcomes must be clearly stated to all concerned.
- Participants will have the knowledge, skills, competencies, experience and information to complete the process or be guided by those who do.
- Managers will want participation to occur.
- Participation will utilise the potential of the participants and will add value to the exercise.
- The solving of problems and the resolution of disputes are best achieved through the active participation of those concerned.

Now answer the following questions.

- Think of a situation in which you have tried to negotiate with someone who has taken an adversarial, headbutting approach and has refused to budge. How might you change your approach if this happens again?
- Consider a conflict that you have witnessed or been part of that was settled by a third party arbitrator who handed down a decision after listening to both sides. Were you satisfied with the outcomes? Could it have been handled in a different manner?
- Under what circumstances could you use a third party mediator to assist the resolution of disputes in your workplace? Who would you select for that role?
- What steps can you now take to foster a joint problem-solving approach to conflict resolution? What training will be required? What other support would assist this change of direction?

activity 17 if and then

When people or groups come at each other from different directions there is potential for conflict. In order for them to come to an agreement it is necessary to change the status quo and for the two sides to converge towards resolution. During the process of negotiation each side will usually consider the other's demands only if they see some of their requests or demands also being taken into consideration. This requires an **if and then** strategy.

> '**If I** were to seriously consider what you are putting to me, **then** I would expect in return that you would...'

The other person replies:
> 'I would only be willing to consider that request **if** you were to agree to...'

Practise this strategy with a colleague, friend, partner or someone you supervise. Practise it first in good fun. Pick a topic that is lighthearted and negotiate an agreement using this approach. When you become more comfortable with the approach start to incorporate it into your more serious negotiations.

Get together with another person and read the case study of Elizabeth and Andrew in Activity 18. You play the role of either Elizabeth or Andrew and the other person plays the other. Using the if and then strategy, negotiate a resolution between Elizabeth and Andrew. The object of the exercise is to resolve their differences using a cooperative problem-solving approach.

Read the case study of Elizabeth and Andrew below. Put yourself in either of their shoes. Charles has told you both to go away and come to a settlement. Use the guide on the following page to assist you to prepare for negotiation and resolution. How would you approach the meeting?

Elizabeth and Andrew

Charles, the Human Resources director of Eastern Distributors Pty Ltd, called Andrew to a meeting to discuss his annual review report, which had been sent to Charles by Elizabeth, the unit manager, with a strong recommendation that Andrew's employment be terminated. Charles read the report that outlined a number of concerns such as lateness; disrupting others; refusal to take advice from three section heads; lack of commitment to company goals and ideals; lack of cooperation; failure to meet the increased 10 per cent target as outlined and agreed upon in the forward plans; and refusal to carry out directions from the manager. Charles informed Andrew that, on the basis of that report, he would have to recommend to the Chief General Manager that he be dismissed, but if he should choose to resign immediately it would be in his own best interests.

Andrew was flabbergasted and became very stressed. He informed Charles that he could not resign. He had just been married and had committed himself to a mortgage on a new house. He informed Charles that he had not seen the report and it had never been discussed with him. Charles told him that the report was quite clear.

Andrew stated that he could not understand the problems because his report last year with the former manager, John, was so glowing. He stated that Elizabeth, since her appointment six months ago, had hardly talked to him even though they had been colleagues before. He suggested that she was jealous because he was the one the staff wanted to become manager when John retired. He admitted to being late on two days but only because his car had broken down. He often talked to other members of staff because he had been appointed as welfare and social officer. Charles informed him that those matters should not disrupt his normal work. Andrew stated that Elizabeth kept shifting him around to different sections and he did not have time to settle down. Charles informed him that this was the new company policy of multiskilling and broadbanding and, as he was obviously having difficulty coping with it, this was further reason for his dismissal.

Andrew explained his inability to reach his annual 10 per cent increase target because he had taken 30 days' long service leave for his honeymoon. He stated that he was not aware of any directions he had failed to carry out. On some occasions Elizabeth had demanded that he cease what he was doing in order to meet urgent requests from the Chief. Charles informed him that it was obvious that he was too inflexible to meet the demands of a modern organisation such as Eastern Distributors.

Exasperated, Andrew informed Charles that he would seek advice and take the matter further.

Charles stated that, in the light of Andrew's concerns, he would ask Elizabeth and Andrew to negotiate some settlement of the issues.

PREPARING FOR NEGOTIATION

- Clarify the issues for you and the other party.
- Seek further information.
- Put yourself in the other person's shoes.
- Establish your top and bottom lines.
- Estimate their top and bottom lines.
- Look to your style of negotiation and their style.
- Clarify any areas of agreement and any unresolved matters.
- Think through a range of options and their implications.
- Estimate their range of options.
- Consider suitable locations and times.
- Consider who should be present and who should not be.
- Be prepared for the unexpected.
- Keep hold of your own agenda.
- Try to calm yourself before each meeting.
- Focus on the desirable process and outcomes.
- Work towards a joint resolution.

You have been asked to investigate a major conflict involving Joe Mustafa and others at an engineering works. Using the following information and the guide on the following page, map the conflict in preparation to deciding how to resolve the issues.

Joe

Joe Mustafa is a process worker at Mercantile Engineering and has been working there for five years. He has been having increasing problems with a Jobset worker. Adri Adrosian has been working beside Joe in order to gain skills, especially related to lathes and presses. Jobset is a scheme that helps young disadvantaged unemployed people to obtain work skills so that they will have a better chance of obtaining full-time work.

Adri complains that Joe picks on him because of his ancestry. Joe contends that Adri and the other Jobset workers vilify him by using rude words in their own native language. Joe reports Adri and the others to the foreman and the production manager almost every day.

George Economides, another worker at the plant, is a skilled toolmaker and sympathises with Adri and the others because he wants to see them get a chance in life. He thinks they would be good workers if treated well. George tells Joe to stop picking on them. In one heated exchange George was heard to say, 'Joe, get back to where you came from, we don't want your kind here.' On another occasion he pushed Joe against the wall and challenged him: 'Have a go at me. Don't pick on the kids. Let's see how good you are with someone my size. Put up or shut up.' Joe left and reported George to the foreman.

The other workers did not want to be involved. In fact, two of them refused to eat in the lunchroom so that they would not become involved. When Joe went to the foreman last week to complain, he was told, 'Look, Joe, you're a bloody good worker and we can't do without you but you have to get on with the others. Take it on the chin, Joe. Learn to smile a bit.' The production manager told him, 'Joe, don't bring your problems to me. You've had enough experience to know what to do. Fix it yourself.'

Joe asked the general manager to visit the shop floor to see how bad the situation was and what the Jobset workers were like. The general manager said that he was too busy running the organisation. 'I pay you good money to look after what goes on in your section. Now get on and do it.'

When the other workers went to the production manager to complain that the constant arguments between Joe, George and the Jobset workers were affecting their work and morale, Fred, the production manager, sent a stern memo to the chief general manager demanding that Joe be sacked or transferred to another site. He warned that if the request were declined, then he knew where the Chief could put the Jobset organisation and everyone associated with it. He reminded the Chief of the quota that he had to maintain and that 'there was no way these turkeys are going to do me out of my annual Christmas bonus by getting behind the targets'.

FIGURE 5.2
Drawing and mapping the conflict

Issues	Information
FACTS	PHOGE
Context/environment	
Main players	Their needs, concerns, anxieties
Other players	Their relationship to each other
Analysis	
Common agreement	
Unresolved matters, hidden agendas	More information needed
Strategies for resolution	
Actions to be taken following agreement	Who is to be involved?
What is the recommended time line?	Monitoring

Conflict in the workplace is initiated often by people whom we consider as difficult. They are the people who get on everyone's nerves; they irritate other workers; they make more than the average number of mistakes; they have mood swings or emotional outbursts beyond acceptable limits; they are disorganised or inefficient and they attack other people.

Earlier in the book I mentioned Dictator Dan, Barbara Blocker and Aggro Andy. Add to that group some of my other favourite characters such as Inefficient Ian, Freda the Fault Finder, Gary Grievance, Fantasy Phil, Hapless Hannah, Cynical Cynthia and Harassing Harry. Most of the people who adopt one of these stereotypical roles will be a cause for concern for you and others in the organisation and in one way or another will initiate much interpersonal conflict.

It is important therefore to address issues emanating from these people as quickly as possible rather than pushing them aside, transferring them or ignoring them.

By yourself or working with a colleague, outline how you will deal with each of these characters when the occasion arises. The object of the exercise is to solve the problems, resolve the issues of concern and to bring these members into a cooperative, cohesive and productive team. Use the points listed below as a guide.

- How will you raise issues of concern with them?
- How will you involve them in the interview?
- How will you change your approach to dealing with them?
- How will you turn their negative, destructive energy into something more positive?
- What strategies will you adopt to improve the outcomes?
- What action will you take to monitor the follow-up?

activity 21 — How will I change my style of operation?

The easiest aspect to change in an environment of conflict is your own approach to managing the situations. It is now important for you to assess how you have traditionally dealt with conflict, disputes and difficult situations and determine how you will now change.

Take time out and reflect on the matters outlined below.

- What have I been doing well and will continue to do in the future?
- Which of these are working so well that I will use them more often than in the past?
- What have I been doing which is useful but not as effective and so will be used less often?
- What will I stop doing because it is not achieving the desired outcome?
- What will I commence using that I have not tried before?
- In general terms, how will I change my approach to dealing with conflict resolution?

■ IN CONCLUSION

Like so many other good things that happen in your life, the creation and maintenance of a conflict-free workplace does not happen overnight — but it will happen if you set your mind to it. Most of you have the potential to become very effective people managers. Be confident that you have the skills, abilities and experience to realise that potential. What you need now is a little courage to experiment with different approaches, to test the edges and push the boundaries into new areas.

In producing this book I have tried to give you the necessary support, guidance and encouragement to try something different. I walk beside you until you can stride ahead with confidence to determine your own direction and destiny.

Remember that you, as change agents, are the most important people in the organisation. I wish you well in your endeavours to improve the work environment for you and those who report to you.

INDEX